MALAYAN POSTSCRIPT

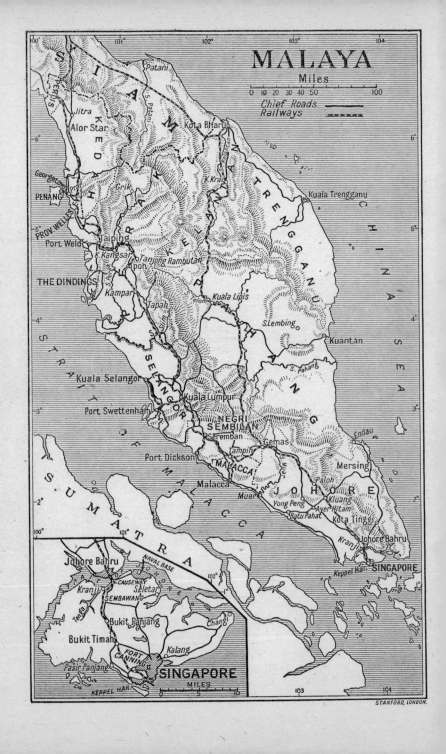

MALAYAN POSTSCRIPT

by

IAN MORRISON

FABER AND FABER LIMITED
24 Russell Square
London

Dedication

Tens of thousands of men, of many races,
fought and bled and died in the Malayan
jungle in an effort that was to prove, through
no fault of their own, vain. This book has been
written in the hope that their effort may not
go entirely unremembered or unhonoured.

BOOK
PRODUCTION
WAR ECONOMY
STANDARD

*This book is produced in complete conformity
with the authorized economy regulations*

*First published in November Mcmxlii
by Faber and Faber Limited
24 Russell Square London W.C.1
Printed in Great Britain by
Western Printing Services Ltd. Bristol*
All Rights Reserved

INTRODUCTION

The Malayan campaign was a unity. It had a dramatic beginning. For nearly all the inhabitants of Singapore it started with the explosion of bombs in the early morning of December 8th. It had an even more dramatic end ten weeks later. After six days of savage fighting on the island of Singapore, over 60,000 men of the British Army, with all their equipment, surrendered to the Japanese. The surrender was the biggest military disaster that has befallen British arms during the last three years. It may prove to have marked the end of an epoch in our imperial history.

It was a disaster. But, mixed up with the disaster, were elements of heroism and sacrifice and tireless effort which should not be forgotten.

The campaign cannot be dismissed, as it is so often dismissed, with one sweeping generalization about official incompetence, or inadequate leadership, or numerical inferiority, or lack of aerial support, or fifth-column activity amongst the natives. The whole thing was complex. Many factors were involved.

The account that follows is a short personal record of the campaign in Malaya. It makes no pretension to being a comprehensive account. The time is still to come for the official histories, with all the relevant documents, official and unofficial, carefully collated. But, if I do not put something down on paper now, I shall never do so. Nearly three months have elapsed since I left the island. Already the events that took place there are becoming dimmed in my memory.

I am not interested in apportioning blame or allotting responsibility for what happened. I am interested in what happened and why it happened. It is precisely those people who are most ignorant of the facts of the Malayan campaign who are most virulent in their attacks and most sweeping in their allegations.

The adjective 'British', which it has become the fashion to employ in contradistinction to 'Australian', will throughout refer to

Introduction

the Imperial forces in Malaya, whether by race they were English, Scottish, Australian, Indian, or Malay.

My thanks are due to *The Times*, for permission to draw on some of the dispatches which I sent them from Malaya; to the War Office, who have kindly undertaken the work of censoring the manuscript, and given me permission to publish this book while I am still a correspondent in the field; to the British Ministry of Information and the Australian Department of Information, for permission to reproduce photographs taken by their official photographers in Malaya; to Yates McDaniel, of the Associated Press, for permission to reproduce some photographs which he took during his eventful voyage from Singapore to Sumatra.

IAN MORRISON

Melbourne, May 1942.

CONTENTS

ILLUSTRATIONS

Illustrations

9

Illustrations

1

THE SINGAPORE LEGEND

It is difficult now to recollect the sense of security that people enjoyed in Singapore during the weeks leading up to the outbreak of war in the Pacific. It seems impossible now that people should have felt safe and happy in a place that was to fall to the enemy so easily.

I came to Singapore in October 1941, two months before war broke out in the Pacific. Previously I had lived in China and Japan. I had travelled in parts of the East which had recently been the scenes of bloody battles. I had known Chungking, a city which Japanese bombers were still trying to bomb into submission. I had lived for two years in Shanghai. Living there was like living on a volcano. At any moment the Japanese might seize upon one particular act of terrorism and make it an excuse for marching into the International Settlement. In other words, I thought of the East as being a troubled part of the world where one could not expect security of any sort. Having lived in Japan I had an inkling of the passions and frustrations that were seething in the breasts of eighty million people.

Singapore, alone of cities in the Far East, gave its inhabitants the illusion of security. Aeroplanes droned overhead during the day. The little Buffalo fighters looked beautifully speedy and manoeuvrable. There was hardly an hour of the day when one looked up into the sky and failed to see an aeroplane of some description—a Blenheim bomber, a Wirraway, a Catalina flying-boat, a torpedo-carrying Wildebeeste. There was frequent fire practice, when the big naval guns that protected the island would hurl their shells many miles out to sea. After nightfall powerful searchlights played over the water or shone upwards into the sky. There were occasional black-out practices. Every Saturday morning the sirens would be tested and would wail piercingly over the city.

The fighting men of many different peoples were to be seen

walking in the streets of Singapore city. Sturdy British infantry-men of famous regiments like the Loyals and the Manchesters; Scottish Highlanders of the Argylls and the Gordons; sunburnt Diggers from Australia; huge bearded Sikhs; Moslem riflemen fresh from service on the North-west Frontier; tough little Gurkhas; Malays of the Malay Regiment; airmen from Britain, Australia, New Zealand; visitors from the Netherlands Air Force in green uniforms; young Chinese who had enlisted in some of the volunteer units—all these different types were to be seen in Singapore. If one went to a cinema, or if one went dancing at Raffles Hotel after dinner, three-quarters of the men would be in uniform. Singapore seemed to be stiff with troops.

On the north-east coast of the island was located the great Naval Base, which had cost over £60,000,000 and taken nearly twenty years to build. Here were twenty-two square miles of deep-sea anchorage, which could accommodate with ease a combined British and American naval force. Here was an enormous floating-dock, towed 8,000 miles from England, large enough for a 45,000-ton battleship; a smaller floating-dock for the repair of destroyers and submarines; a graving-dock, which could accommodate, with a few feet to spare, the *Queen Mary* or the *Queen Elizabeth*. Here was a giant crane which could lift an entire gun turret out of a battleship; workshops for the repair and servicing of machinery and guns; wharves for revictualling and refuelling ships; huge underground oil and armament depots; an Admiralty transmit-ting station that was one of the most powerful in the world; shore establishments for the crews of ships. The Naval Base was a little world of its own. Rivers had been diverted that it might come into being. Much of the land had been reclaimed from the sea. It was shut off from the world by a high palisade of barbed wire. The gates were jealously guarded. Whole residential areas inside the palisade housed the men who worked at the base. There were cinemas, churches, seventeen football fields.

Here also at the Naval Base was the brain-centre and nerve-centre of British strategy in the Far East. Large office buildings housed the staffs of Vice-Admiral Sir Geoffrey Layton, Com-mander-in-Chief of the China Squadron, and Air Chief-Marshal Sir Robert Brooke-Popham, Commander-in-Chief, Far East, whose command extended over the military and aerial forces of Malaya, Burma, Hong Kong, and British Borneo. The latter especially was held in considerable esteem as a man who was a hustler despite his seniority. On the outskirts of the city were the headquarters of Mr. Duff Cooper, who had come out to the Far East on a mission for the British Government and was later to be appointed British Resident Cabinet Minister in the Far East.

With all these superficial indications of power, it is easy to see how people could feel safe and happy in Singapore. They saw many different uniforms in the streets. Therefore they thought we had enough soldiers. They saw aeroplanes in the sky. Therefore we were strong enough in the air. We had a marvellous Naval Base. Therefore we had nothing to fear at sea. By October 1941 the Singapore legend was really well established. British and American newspapermen had visited Singapore and written glowing articles about it. British statesmen had talked confidently about its strength. It had become the fashion to refer to it as 'the fortress of Singapore', or, often, as 'the impregnable fortress of Singapore'. The legend had already achieved a world-wide currency.

A few people, after they had been in Singapore a short time, began to realize that Singapore's strength was potential rather than actual. Amazing strides had admittedly been made during the past eighteen months. If Japan had come into the war at the time of the fall of France, we should not have been in a position to contest a Japanese advance down the mainland at all. We could only have attempted to defend the island. That dangerous moment passed. Both troops and equipment began to flow into Singapore in a steady stream. Nevertheless, in October 1941 there were still certain grave deficiencies. There were virtually no ships. Despite the continuous drone of aeroplanes over Singapore Island, there were not enough aeroplanes. There were no tanks. There were very few anti-tank guns. There were not enough anti-aircraft guns. But we hoped, and indeed assumed, that these things would come. We envisaged a war with Japan developing along the following lines. On the outbreak of hostilities British and American naval units would at once begin to assemble in the south-west Pacific. They would challenge the Japanese control of those sea-routes which would be essential to any attack launched against either Malaya or the Netherlands East Indies. There would be an immediate accretion of air strength. British fighter planes would fly eastwards from the Middle East and from India, using the chain of secret jungle airfields which had been prepared for them all the way from India, across Burma, down the Malayan penin-sula, to Singapore. Heavy American bombers would fly across the Pacific and then up from Australia to Singapore. We expected the Japanese to attempt landings on the east coast, at Kota Bahru, Endau, and Mersing. But it ought to be possible to repulse these attempts without difficulty. It was known that fixed defences had been erected on those beaches where the enemy might be expected to land. Certain Indian formations had specialized in repelling attempted landings. The idea of an overland invasion of Malaya down the length of the peninsula was not one that we took very seriously. The Japanese would have to bring all their supplies by sea across the Gulf of Siam. They would not be allowed to do this with impunity. Even if they did succeed in securing a foothold in the north, it ought to be possible, surely, for the British forces to straddle the narrow neck of the peninsula and prevent any south-ward advance by the overland route. Besides, there was our ally the jungle, the 'impenetrable' jungle, as many people, who had never tried to penetrate it, were in the habit of calling it. As for a siege of Singapore or an assault on the island from the landward side, these possibilities belonged to the realm of remote specu-lation.

The important thing about Singapore was that an allied naval force, and an allied air force, could operate from it in the event of an emergency in the western Pacific. All the facilities were ready and waiting. This was the line which the Ministry of Information in Singapore took with the British and American correspondents who began to pass through Singapore in a steady stream at the beginning of 1941. There was no deliberate attempt on the part of our official publicists to 'sell' Singapore to the world. The em-phasis was on the potential, not on the actual. But the world wanted to be sold Singapore. It wanted to believe that Singapore was an impregnable fortress, a bulwark against Japanese aggres-sion in the Pacific. Gradually the transference was made from

The Singapore Legend

potential to actual. The distinction became blurred in the public, and also, to a large extent, in the official, mind. The legend grew. It was fostered, during the six months before the war actually broke out, by the propaganda line which we began to take *vis-à-vis* the Japanese. At the time of the fall of France they had marched into northern Indo-China. In the summer of 1941 they had marched into southern Indo-China, where they secured an ideal base for launching attacks east against the Philippines, south-east against the Netherlands East Indies, south against Malaya, or west against Thailand and Burma. They were now subjecting the Thais to increasing pressure. At any moment they might march into Thailand. Thailand was in Asia what Poland had been in Europe—the point where a British government finally decided to say 'Stop'. Therefore British statesmen said in their public utterances: 'We do not want war with you Japanese. But if you want it we are ready for it. It is entirely up to you whether there is war or not.'

Our service chiefs, and also the general public, felt genuinely confident. We had come to believe our own propaganda. We knew also that the American public was more psychologically prepared for positive action against Japan than against Germany. We knew that Japan's economy was rapidly deteriorating. From this economic weakness we inferred military weakness.

There were, however, a few observers who were not altogether content with the popular estimate of Singapore's strength. In July 1941 there appeared some remarkable diagrams in the American magazine *Life* with explanatory paragraphs based on reports by my friend Teddy White, showing how, in the event of war, the Japanese navy would attempt to smash the American fleet at Pearl Harbour and the Japanese army would try to fight its way down the west coast of Malaya. There was Cecil Brown of Columbia Broadcasting System, who, during the months before the outbreak of war, played the role of Cassandra, inveighing against the 'it-can't-happen-here' attitude of the British in Malaya. (This true prophet eventually had his British War Office accreditation taken away from him on the grounds that his broadcasts to America, which could also be picked up in Malaya, were having a depressing effect on local morale. It created considerable stir at the time. Brown had the unanswerable case that he had never once broadcast anything that had not been passed by the local censorship.) Brown's forebodings had less effect on the public than they might have had. People were never quite sure how far they were based on a balanced and dispassionate estimate of the situation, how far they were the product of a bilious and habitually critical temper. The gloomy prophets like Brown, however, were voices crying in the wilderness. They failed to disturb the sense of security in which Singapore and its inhabitants basked.

Two things happened during the weeks before the actual declaration of hostilities that tended to confirm this sense of security. The first was the arrival in Hong Kong of two battalions of Canadian troops. The public felt that the British Government would not have troubled to reinforce the garrison at this northern outpost unless it was determined to hold the island in the event of an attack, and unless it felt that the island could be held. Besides, the arrival of Canadians, men who stand half-way between the British and the Americans, seemed in some indefinable way to increase America's stake in the Far East. When the news was first released, it had a tonic effect out of all proportion to its purely military significance.

The second event was the arrival at Singapore, during the week before the outbreak of war, of the *Prince of Wales* and the *Repulse* accompanied by destroyers. This squadron was to be the nucleus of a new Far Eastern fleet under the command of Vice-Admiral Sir Tom Phillips. With what mingled emotions we watched the two ships as they steamed majestically to their anchorage off the Naval Base! Those strange grey shapes on the skyline, they were symbols of our new-found strength, concrete expressions of the confidence with which we faced any emergency that might arise in the Pacific. Singapore's potential naval significance was at last becoming reality.

It was in such a mood as this that the inhabitants of Singapore and Malaya waited to see what the month of December 1941 would bring forth.

2

DREAM AND REALITY

Singapore was an island. But that did not make it a fortress. And indeed, only in the strictest sense of the term was it an island. It was surrounded by water. But essentially the island was a continuation of the mainland. Before the start of the campaign, and right up to the day the Japanese set foot on the island, the Straits of Johore were commonly regarded as a natural defensive barrier. Too late did people perceive that the Straits were only what every river, creek, and swamp on the mainland had been to the enemy—not an obstacle but a route, a main avenue of penetration.

Badly as the correspondents may have misunderstood the situation in Malaya before the beginning of hostilities, there were few who, once hostilities had got well under way, preserved their illusions, least of all about Singapore being a 'fortress'. Once the Imperial forces had failed to hold the Japanese in Johore, it seemed that nothing on earth could save Singapore. Compare Singapore with some of the other fortresses and beleaguered cities of this war. Hong Kong at least had the natural qualifications of a fortress in that rocky mass that juts so sharply out of the sea. Malta at least had deep shelters where the civil population could take cover. Tobruk at least contained only a garrison. The commanders did not have a large civilian population to worry about all the time. Moscow at least had a civilian population animated by a fierce spirit of resistance. But Singapore had none of these things. It was an expanse of low-lying land that had no natural aid to offer its defenders. It had no deep air-raid shelters for its population and not enough shallow shelters. The task of its defenders was complicated by the presence of an enormous Asiatic population that felt it had little stake in the struggle that was taking place. Even the presence of a large number of armed men, together with considerable equipment, was not sufficient to turn this expanse of reclaimed mangrove swamp into a fortress. Singapore was not a fortress. It was a naval base.

Sir Stamford Raffles first perceived the enormous strategical significance of Singapore's geographical position. This significance was threefold:

Firstly, the country that controls Singapore controls the main shipping route between Europe and Asia, the main channel between the Indian and Pacific oceans. There are other routes, it is true: Sunda Strait (between Sumatra and Java), Bali Strait (between Java and Bali), Macassar Strait (between Borneo and Celebes), the Molucca Passage (between Celebes and Halmahera), Torres Straits (between New Guinea and Australia), Bass Strait (between Australia and Tasmania), the Tasman Sea (between Australia and New Zealand). But these other routes are either unnecessarily difficult or unnecessarily circuitous. The obvious ocean channel between east and west is the channel to the south of Singapore. It is formed of the Malacca Strait (between Sumatra and the Malayan peninsula) to the west and the south China Sea to the east.

Secondly, the country that controls Singapore is in a position to dominate strategically, and to a large extent economically, that rich area comprising Malaya and the Indies which is undoubtedly the richest purely colonial area in the world. Oil, tin, rubber, tea, coal, iron, rice, quinine, kapok, copra, spices—what commodity is there that cannot be found in these islands, in the greatest abundance, with a supply of cheap, industrious, and docile labour close at hand?.

Thirdly, the Straits of Johore form one of the best natural harbours in the south-west Pacific area.

These three things give Singapore its tremendous significance in world affairs. For these three reasons, Singapore was a pearl of great price in the British Empire. For these three reasons, its loss to the Japanese was a disaster of the first magnitude. But it is important to be quite clear on one point. *Control presupposes the means of control.* When we say 'the country that controls Singapore' we must remember that that control implies something more than mere possession or occupation. It cannot be enforced without the battleships, the destroyers, the submarines, the long-range bombers, the fighter planes, the land forces, all of which must be based on Singapore and operate from it.

During the last century Great Britain exercised that control because, in an unchallenged mastery of the sea, she possessed the means of control. Even if there were no ships at all at Singapore, they could eventually be concentrated in that theatre of war and any threat successfully disposed of.

The first two decades of the present century saw the gradual rise of Japan, under the tutelage of Great Britain, to the status of a first-class power. British advisers and experts, ironically enough, played very much the same role then that Nazi advisers and experts are playing to-day. Already, with the acquisition of Korea, the serving of the Twenty-one Demands on China, and the Siberian venture of 1921, Japan's aspirations to domination of the continental mainland and her dreams of a widespread Pacific empire were becoming apparent for all the world to see. After the Great War we scrapped the Anglo-Japanese Alliance and substituted for it the Nine-Power Treaty. The latter was really an attempt to stabilize and perpetuate the *status quo* in Asia and the Pacific. At the same time British statesmen pondered what more concrete measures might usefully be taken to achieve this stabilization. Eventually they decided, in the early twenties, upon the construction of a great naval base at Singapore.

The task of protecting against enemy attack the eastern portions of the British Empire—Hong Kong, Malaya, Singapore, British Borneo, New Guinea, Australia, New Zealand, the Pacific islands, Burma, India—was at that time regarded primarily as the responsibility of the British Navy. The construction of a large naval base, from which the British fleet could operate in the Pacific, very possibly aided by, and by no stretch of the imagination opposed by, the French and American fleets, seemed to be the best means of countering any attempt on the part of Japan to extend her influence to the point where it conflicted with the vital interests of the British Empire. It was wise long-term policy, and the base was eventually completed in 1939. But certain things happened in the interim which did not completely harmonize with the original strategic conceptions of the planners and designers of the naval base. Chief of these new factors was the development of the air arm.

The whole British strategic concept of Singapore depended upon certain conditions which, when it came to the test, were either only partially fulfilled or else not fulfilled at all. The defence of the eastern portions of the British Empire, including Singapore, was regarded, as emphasized above, as being the responsibility of the British Navy. The only two capital ships we were able to spare in December 1941 from our grave preoccupations in the Atlantic and the Mediterranean were sunk by the Japanese three days after the war began. The United States Pacific fleet, from which so much had been hoped, was temporarily eliminated from the conflict in the devastating Japanese attack on Pearl Harbour on the first morning of war. The French fleet had, of course, ceased to be a factor in the situation after the French capitulation to Germany in the summer of 1940. Thus three days after the outbreak of hostilities the enemy had gained an almost complete naval superiority in the Pacific and the defenders of Singapore had to do their best with practically no naval support except that which our Dutch allies could give us. Knocked clean away, in the opening round of the war, was the main prop on which the defence of Singapore rested. Nor was the situation in the air very much better. The Japanese occupation of Victoria Point, and later of Mergui (both in Tenasserim, in southernmost Burma), meant that no fighter planes could thenceforward be flown direct from the Middle East or India to Malaya. Reinforcements of fighter planes would have to come, as they did come, by sea in crates. Moreover, for a variety of reasons, which will be described in detail later, the Japanese early in the campaign secured a mastery in the air that was almost unchallenged. Our small army, originally intended to defend an island roughly the same size and shape as the Isle of Wight, found itself called upon to defend an area the size of England and Wales, with negligible assistance at sea and negligible assistance in the air.

Singapore was not a fortress. It was a naval base. In other words, it was a station to which naval units, after taking part in offensive

operations against an enemy, could return in order to revictual
and refuel, rest their personnel, and repair any damage that had
been suffered.

The possibility of a landward assault on the island was not one
that seems to have occurred to the planners of Singapore, who
were planning at a time when the nearest Japanese base was
Formosa (1,520 miles away), not Saigon (648 miles away). They
envisaged only an assault from the sea. Therefore the naval base
and all important installations were placed on the landward, i.e.
the northern, shore of the island. Huge naval guns embedded in
concrete foundations pointed out to sea. It is very possible, indeed
probable, that Singapore was impregnable against an attack
launched from the sea. In the same way the Maginot Line was
almost certainly impregnable against direct assault launched from
the east. But unfortunately the Maginot Line was never assaulted
from the east, nor was Singapore attacked from the sea.

Twenty years later the possibility of a landward assault on the
island was very definitely in the minds of the military commanders
of Singapore. They were prepared to have to fight a campaign on
the mainland, but also they expected that the Japanese would try
to land only at points on the east coast of the peninsula. There
were three points of danger on the east coast: Kota Bahru, Kuantan, and Mersing. From Kota Bahru there is a road as far as Kuala
Krai, and then a railway that runs south through the centre of the
peninsula. From Kuantan there is a road that runs due west across
the peninsula. From Mersing there is a road that runs south-west
one hundred miles to Singapore. All these points were defended.
The enemy, however, only landed at one of them, namely, at
Kota Bahru. The training of certain of the British units was
devoted almost entirely to practice in repelling enemy landing
operations. The possibility of a Japanese advance down the *west*
coast of Malaya, although in the minds of our commanders, does
not appear to have been as seriously considered by them as the
possibility of an advance starting at points on the east coast. They
were counting on our combined military, naval, and air forces
being able to prevent the Japanese from ever gaining a base on the
peninsula from which to advance down the west coast. It was the
possession of Singora in south Thailand that enabled the Japanese

to fight a campaign down the west coast. Their transports crossed the Gulf of Siam from Saigon with comparative impunity. Submarines of the Royal Netherlands Navy sank a few of them in the early stages, but that was all. There were never enough British bombers even to make things at Singora moderately hot for the Japanese. The main Japanese base for their campaign in Malaya was not bombed more than once, and then only by a small formation of British bombers.

The basic assumptions made by the original planners of Singapore and by the military defenders at a later date gave birth to other assumptions which were no less erroneous and no less disastrous. Because they were expecting either an assault on Singapore from the sea or landings on the peninsula which could be repelled on the beaches, there were no fixed or even prepared defences in Malaya beyond the big shore batteries on the island and the beach defences at Kota Bahru, Kuantan, Mersing, and one or two other points. Penang had exactly two six-inch guns. There were no measures taken in advance on the west coast, no rubber plantations cleared to give fields of fire, no tank traps, no gun emplacements. There were no pill-boxes, no prepared positions on the northern coast of the island overlooking the Straits of Johore. Our forces eventually tried to repel the Japanese attack on the island from behind the protection afforded by barbed wire, sandbags, shallow rifle-pits, and whatever other measures could be hastily improvised. Moreover, one cannot help wondering if the study of the terrain made by our military commanders had not been somewhat defective. Tanks, they believed, would never be able to operate over this jungle-covered country. The Dutch High Command refused to accept Singapore's estimate of the tank question, experimented with tanks, found that they could play a role in operations in Java, purchased some from America and took measures to counter their use by the enemy.

Such were some of the assumptions on which the defence of Singapore ultimately rested, assumptions which were blown sky-high during the first week of the war.

3

THE FACTUAL BACKGROUND

There are certain essential facts about Malaya and Singapore which anyone wishing to understand the campaign that was fought there must know.

At its narrowest point, on the Thai border, the Malayan peninsula is some 100 miles across, at its widest point it is some 200 miles across. From the Thai border to the south-easterly tip of the mainland is a distance of approximately 450 miles. The Japanese covered this distance at the remarkable speed of just under nine miles per day.

The island of Singapore (twenty-eight miles from east to west, fourteen from south to north) is roughly the same size and shape as the Isle of Wight. In relation to the Malayan mainland the area of the island is roughly as the Isle of Wight is to England and Wales. It does not have, however, the steep cliffs of the Isle of Wight and it is much closer to the mainland. It is separated from the mainland by the Straits of Johore which average less than one mile in width. The one link with the mainland is the famous Johore causeway, completed in 1924, exactly 1,155 yards in length and averaging sixteen yards in width at low tide, carrying a road, two lines of rails, and large water mains.

A range of granite mountains forms the backbone of the peninsula. Subsidiary ranges run parallel to it in a general south-easterly direction. East and west there are coastal plains, the western coastline being largely composed of mangrove swamps, the eastern coastline of sandy beaches fringed with palms and casuarina trees. Conspicuous landmarks on the plains are the great limestone bluffs which jut upwards in an unexpected fashion.

Except where man has been at work Malaya is still one vast tropical forest. Over 72 per cent of the terrain is jungle. Decaying vegetable matter, basted by a tropical sun, drenched by torrential rainfall, forms a most fertile soil. The jungle, which springs from it, is composed of many growths—huge tropical trees; groves and thickets of bamboo; palms and ferns; parasitic creepers, which mount the taller trees, form thick hawsers, and eventually throttle their hosts; exquisite orchids of a thousand varieties; flowering creepers of many kinds; banana-trees, with six-foot leaves, bearing different kinds of fruit, some small and yellow, some long and green, some large and red; huge ferns nestling in the forks of trees, trailing vines, rare mosses. And then the tropical fruit—durians, with a peculiar pungent odour, whose flesh the Malays hold to be an aphrodisiac; coconuts, whose milk they hold to have a contrary effect upon the system; jack-fruit, like overgrown vegetable marrows hanging from the trees; delicious little mango-steens, tastiest of them all; rambutans, whose skin is covered with red spines; and many others. The jungle is a marvellously beautiful, but somehow rather terrifying, place. There are two important things to note about it as far as the war was concerned. It is laced by rivers, streams, and creeks, up and down which the Malays travel on rafts of bamboo poles tied together with rattan. Water is one of the chief methods of inland travel. Secondly, although the jungle itself is often 'impenetrable', nevertheless there are many jungle paths and tracks all over the peninsula, known to the Malay hunters and villagers and those who have made a study of the terrain.

Where the jungle has been cleared by man, it is usually for the purpose of planting rubber. The rubber plantations stretch for acre after acre over much of the peninsula, especially on the west coast. The trees are planted at regular intervals and are cicatrized with a scar where the tapping is done. If one just cuts the bark with a penknife, it begins to ooze a pure white liquid. This liquid, when it first comes out, is not sticky at all, but it develops elastic qualities when it congeals. Certain things are also worth noting about the rubber plantations. First, they provided good cover from the air. How many times did we not lie on our stomachs beneath rubber trees, while Japanese dive-bombers circled around overhead, their attention aroused by something suspicious in the foliage below! The trees saved our lives on numerous occasions. Secondly, the intervals at which the rubber trees are planted are sufficiently wide to admit of the passage of a tank. Moreover all the rubber estates are equipped with excellent metalled roads since the managers were making increasing use of motor transport. Thirdly, the rubber trees burn with difficulty. People often ask why the scorched earth policy was not enforced more rigorously in Malaya. As far as the rubber was concerned, the policy was enforced by burning the stocks of latex and by destroying machinery. But it was not possible to dispose of the millions of trees on the rubber estates. They were too green to burn, and it would have taken several years to cut them all down. (The rubber tree was imported into Malaya from Brazil via Kew Gardens about 1880. The rubber industry only began to assume its present proportions at the beginning of the present century. It was brought into being very largely by the development of the motor-car. Now that artificial rubber, more durable than the natural rubber, is being produced on a large scale in the United States and elsewhere, it is interesting to speculate on the chances of survival of Malaya's primary industry. Before the expansion of the rubber industry, coffee was the main product of Malaya.)

The other source of Malaya's wealth is tin, Malaya produced nearly half the world's yield of tin ore. It also produced more than half the yield of smelted tin, since much tin was brought into Malaya for smelting from Banka and other islands in the Netherlands East Indies. Amongst the greatest deep tin-mines in the world are those at Sungei Lembing on the east coast near Kuantan. Driving up to the front line on the west coast we used to see many tin-mines. The great mounds of washed alluvial soil were a conspicuous feature of the landscape.

All sorts of animals live in the jungle of Malaya—tigers, leopards, bison, tapirs, elephants, deer, gibbons, and many others. Despite an inveterate interest in natural history I saw few wild animals during my four months in Malaya. A large monitor lizard up a tree, some monkeys scampering across a road, a peacock in a jungle glade—that was all. The majority of newspapermen could never refer to a swamp or a creek without prefixing the adjective 'crocodile-infested'. They have one specimen over seventeen feet long in the Raffles Museum at Singapore. It was caught on Singapore Island. The longest recorded specimen was a monster over thirty-two feet long. But during all those weeks, when both the enemy and ourselves were swimming and wading across swamps and creeks, I never once heard of a crocodile attacking a man or even of a crocodile being seen. The same applied to sharks. The waters of the south-west Pacific are supposed to be alive with sharks. The Timor Sea especially is invariably described as 'shark-infested'. But amongst all the cases in which ships were sunk and men thrown into the sea, in the Timor Sea as well as in other waters round Malaya and the Indies, I never once heard of a man being attacked by a shark or of a shark being seen.

There was a curious thing about the fishing situation in Malaya, which I will mention here as we have strayed on to the subject of fish. Excellent fish were to be had in Singapore in peacetime, but the fishing was done almost entirely by Japanese fishermen. During the months before the outbreak of war many of these men left Malaya with the assistance of the Japanese authorities. Later doubtless they played an important part as guides to the Japanese forces. Those who remained were interned on the outbreak of hostilities. The result was that there were few fishermen left. The Japanese, however, continued to provide the island with fish. Whenever they bombed the big air base at Seletar or the civil airport at Kalang several of their bombs were certain to fall into the sea. Hundreds of fish would be blown to the surface and later collected, chiefly by Chinese, who sold them in the markets at high prices.

Malaya during the weeks of the campaign was hot during the day, but not hot enough to necessitate a sun helmet, unless you were an old British resident. Although only a few miles from the Equator, many people never wore a hat in Singapore, and one rarely heard of a case of sunstroke. It used to become sufficiently chilly at night for a blanket to be desirable. Shortly before the war began the British troops had their cumbersome Wellesley helmets changed for the more sensible broad-brimmed rough-rider hats which the Australian forces always wear. One result of this change was that in the early days of the campaign the Japanese thought that they were being opposed by Australian troops. Tokyo radio used to broadcast fantastic claims as to the number of Australian prisoners they had taken. The error may have been deliberate in order to find out where the Australians were, but it was more probably produced by this change in headgear. The Australian troops used to wear nothing but shorts and most of them were beautifully bronzed. One British officer, cut off from his unit in the fighting round Muar and obliged to make his way back through the jungle, happened to spy some naked torsos through the trees. He gave out a loud shout of welcome, because as he told me, 'I thought they could only be Australians'. Unfortunately they turned out to be Japanese. The British officer only just succeeded in getting away from them. On the whole the Australians seemed to me to stand up to the climate better than the other white troops, perhaps because they come from a warmer country. For some curious reason the British Tommy in the tropics, far from getting bronzed, tends to go a bright lobster pink. The Australians were also harder trained than most of the English and Scottish units. Those units, however, like the Argylls, whose training had been especially severe, stood up to the climate just as well as the Australians.

The climate of Malaya, whether it is because of the heat or the humidity, definitely seems to have a softening effect upon those white people who spend their lives in the country. It seems difficult for a white man in that climate to preserve the energy with which he sets out on his career. There is often a gradual closing-up of his intellectual horizon. He tends to lapse into that genial atmosphere of easygoing *bonhomie* in which so many white men in the tropics like to spend their social hours. Perhaps it was the heat that was responsible. Perhaps it was the humidity, about which people often complained. Certainly white children used to look pale and unwell. Perhaps, on the other hand, it was the life of the white man in Malaya, necessitating little struggle and little effort, which brought about this eventual softening. It was a phenomenon which puzzled me, for the Dutch in the Indies, living in a climate that is even hotter and more humid, did not appear to suffer from it to the same extent. (Are the Japanese likely to suffer from it? Is it the fate of virile races from the north to lose their virility in warm southern climes? These are questions one would like to be able to answer.)

As for communications, there was one railway which ran north

The Factual Background

from Singapore up to the west coast to Thailand. One loop left the main line in Johore, and ran up the centre of the peninsula until it rejoined the main line in the north again. There was a good trunk road all down the west coast, but there were few roads on the east coast, where communications were bad. Roads from Kuantan and Mersing on the east coast ran westwards to join the main network in the west. In the west there were good roads round all the larger towns in addition to the numerous estate roads.

At first glance at the map of Malaya one might think that any campaign would have been fought down the east coast, since this was the coast nearest to the Japanese bases. But all the good communications were down the west coast, and it was down the west coast that the campaign was fought.

The total population of Malaya (including Singapore) was estimated in December 1938, to amount to 5,278,866 persons. The racial pattern was as follows:

Chinese	2,220,244
Malays	2,210,867
Indians	743,555
Europeans	28,211
Aboriginals	30,000
Eurasians	18,310
Japanese	7,951
Miscellaneous	19,728

At the time of the last decennial census in 1931 the population of Singapore numbered 567,000, composed as follows:

Chinese	422,000
Malays	71,000
Indians	51,000
Europeans	8,000
Eurasians	7,000

At that time 74·3 per cent of the population of Singapore were Chinese, 12·5 per cent were Malays, 9·0 per cent were Indians. In 1938 the population of Singapore was estimated to

28

have increased from 567,000 to 720,200, and the percentage of Chinese had still further increased.

The reactions to the war of the different sections of this polyglot population will be described in detail later. The following are some of their outstanding characteristics.

The Malays, who have given their name to the peninsula and whose language is a *lingua franca* amongst all classes, are of southern Mongoloid stock and do not look unlike the Japanese. The Japanese took advantage of this likeness. It was to prove an important factor in the campaign. The Malays are a courteous, good-mannered people; loving pleasure and hating hard work; professing Mohammedanism, to which they were converted in the fourteenth and fifteenth centuries, but not particularly religious; indolent and improvident; not brave, although capable of bravery, and not warlike, although in the past addicted to warfare, and not interested in money, although inveterate gamblers. There was little Malay nationalism, and Malaya was an easy place to administer compared with India and Burma.

The 2,220,244 Chinese in Malaya came chiefly from Canton, Hainan Island, Foochow, and Amoy. A variety of motives have made the Chinese one of the greatest, if perhaps the least known, colonizing powers of the world. Over nine million Chinese live in the countries that border China—Indo-China, Thailand, Malaya, Burma, the Indies—urged abroad by the lure of commerce, by their spirit of enterprise, by the desperate overcrowding of many areas of China, and at certain periods by unsettled conditions in their native land. It was the Chinese who really ran Malaya. They had made it what it was quite as much as had the British. There is much to be said for the theory that the campaign in Malaya was fought ultimately to decide, not whether the British or the Japanese should be the future masters of Malaya, but whether the Japanese or the Chinese should be the masters. Chinese labourers provided all the labour in the tin-mines and much of the labour on the estates. Chinese shopkeepers formed the merchant middle-class. Chinese capitalists, some on a large and some on a small scale, had played a big part in the development of the tin and rubber industries. Under a benevolent British administration much wealth passed into their hands. There were millionaires,

like the incredible Mr. Aw Boon Haw, who started life as a coolie
and ended as a Croesus, manufacturer of that famous salve 'Tiger
Balm' which is found throughout the length and breadth of the
Far East, a cure-all which can be taken in any fashion. Nearly all
the Chinese immigrants into Malaya came from the poor classes in
China. Malaya was for them what America was for Europeans in
the last century, a land where the poorest man might rise to great
heights of wealth and prosperity. Foreigners used to make a distinction between the Straits-born and the China-born Chinese.
The reactions of the two classes will be studied later. Many of the
Straits-born Chinese had lived in Malaya for several generations,
intermarried with the Malays, forgotten their original tongue, and
spoke English or Malay instead. But if they had lost some of the
outward characteristics of the Chinese, they preserved all the
industry, the enterprise, the peasant shrewdness of their country-
men.

The Chinese were the most politically conscious of the three
main native communities. Most of the Indians (except for the
merchants) were too poor and illiterate, the Malays too apathetic,
to have any political views or sympathies. The Chinese, on the
other hand, even when they were not political followers of the
Kuomintang or Communist parties, took a keen interest in political developments in the Far East. They knew what was going on
in the world. They realized all the implications of the struggle
that was now in progress.

There were more Chinese than Malays in Malaya. Singapore
was essentially a Chinese city. In 1911 the Malays formed 53 per
cent of the total population of Malaya, in 1921 49·2 per cent, in
1931 45·0 per cent. This steady decline took place despite an increase in the numbers of Malays in Malaya, mostly as a result of
Malay immigration from south Thailand. The Malays felt that
they were being swamped by the Chinese and dispossessed by
them. As a result they bore considerable hostility towards them.
This was a cardinal factor in deciding the attitude of the Malay
population towards the conflict. Their hostility towards the Chinese
made them, if not sympathetic, then at any rate indifferent, towards the Japanese. Exactly the same thing has happened in
Burma. Fear of the Chinese, even more than dislike of the British,

has made many sections of Burma's population side actively with the Japanese. In Malaya there seemed to exist an unspoken alliance between the British and the Chinese. The Chinese were more industrious than the Malays, more intelligent, more enterprising. The British found them more useful partners than the Malays in developing Malaya, The alliance was reinforced latterly by developments in the political field which made Great Britain and China allies in the same struggle. Many Malays felt that the British had sold their country out to the Chinese. A leading Malay citizen of Singapore, while tolerant of the British, was extremely bitter towards the Chinese. If the Japanese are left in control of Malaya, it is probable that their administration will veer in the other direction and will favour the Malays at the expense of the Chinese, both because the Malays are already sympathetic towards them and because enmity between the Japanese and the Chinese is now so fundamental and deep-seated. 'Asia for the Asiatics' (where it does not mean 'Asia for the Japanese') will be construed in Malaya as 'Malaya for the Malays'. But it is worth noting, for those who feel that the Malays have been given a raw deal by the British, that the Malays themselves are comparative newcomers to their country. They dispossessed still earlier aboriginal inhabitants, who are still to be found in little settlements chiefly on the west coast.

The Indians were of two types. There were many Hindu merchants in Singapore, most of them loyal to Congress. But the vast majority were Tamils from South India, the overflow of those densely crowded areas round Madras, supplying the cheap manual labour that was required on the rubber estates, at the docks, on the railways, in the cities. They were the poorest section of the population, the men clad usually only in a loincloth, the women heavily ornamented with cheap jewellery, the children absolutely sweet with a look of preternatural wisdom in their dark eyes. They were very hard workers, nearly always illiterate, ardent devotees of their religious cults, keeping to themselves, and not marrying with any of the other peoples.

There was also an influential Arab merchant class in Singapore whose political outlook was swayed largely by political developments in the Middle East.

The Factual Background

The 7,900 Japanese in Malaya were to be found in a limited number of professions. There were the fishermen already referred to. There were some large Japanese iron-mines up in Trengganu and Johore and a limited number of rubber estates under Japanese ownership. All these concerns employed Japanese staffs. Then there were Japanese photographers, dentists, masseurs, and small shopkeepers. In almost every town or village of any consequence throughout Malaya there were one or two Japanese shops—usually M. Sakai, photographer, or Y. Goto, general goods store. Some of these men were undoubtedly agents who had been planted. It would be found that certain of the photographers were remarkably keen on hunting and shooting, spending much time in the jungle, and contriving to live securely despite a small volume of business in the photographic line. They used to encourage the troops to bring films to their shops for developing at specially cheap rates. Nearly all of these Japanese residents in Malaya were undoubtedly used by the Japanese intelligence services, more often as sources of information than as instruments of subversive propaganda. Later of course in the actual campaign their specialized knowledge of the terrain proved most useful. Japanese agents in Malaya were secretly in touch with certain of the disaffected members of the Malay ruling houses and with Indian nationalists. They also made use of a subterranean Chinese intelligence organization, run by partisans of the Wang Ching-wei puppet government, but ultimately controlled by, and reporting to, the Japanese. (Madam Wang Ching-wei was a Straits-born Chinese, hailing, if I remember rightly, from Singapore. She was a woman who exerted a great influence on her husband.) Many of the Singapore Chinese came from Hainan and remitted their earnings to Hainan, an island which had been occupied by the Japanese in 1938. The Japanese would often secure the co-operation of Chinese agents by blackmailing them and threatening to bring pressure to bear on their dependants in China.

Throughout the campaign in Malaya, Japanese Intelligence was extremely good. It was equally good in other theatres of war. Only the most perfect Intelligence could have enabled the initial attack on Pearl Harbour to do so much damage. Our officials in Malaya suspected the existence of a widespread organization and

32

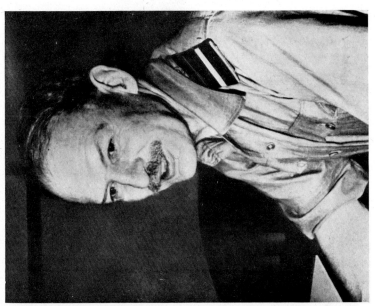

Air Chief-Marshal Sir Robert Brooke-Popham,
Commander-in-Chief, Far East, 1941

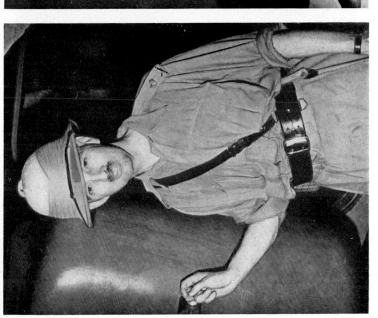

Lieutenant-General A. E. Percival,
G.O.C. British Forces in Malaya

General Wavell in Malaya

Lieutenant-General Sir Henry Pownall

indeed had a large number of the leaders under surveillance. It may be asked why we did not take further steps to curb potentially dangerous activities. The answer is, I suppose, that if you are going to administer a country on democratic lines, something more than suspicion is required before you interfere with the legitimate activities of immigrants. To be completely safe in Malaya, it would have been necessary to keep all Japanese out of the country. There was a further point. Whereas in checking subversive activities by Indians and Chinese, our officials could always get Indians and Chinese to work against their fellow-countrymen, this was never possible in the case of the Japanese, who were bound together by race as by some Masonic fraternity.

British Malaya consisted of three classes of territory. First, there were the Straits Settlements, consisting of Singapore, Malacca, and Penang. These were the settlements whose acquisition eventually led to the extension of British control over the mainland. None of them was acquired by force of arms. Singapore was *purchased* in 1819 from the Sultan of Johore, when it was an island covered in jungle and mangrove swamp, inhabited only by a few native fishermen. Penang was *purchased* from the Sultan of Kedah in 1786. Malacca had been taken by force of arms from the Dutch in 1795 but was returned to them in 1818 and then, six years later, exchanged for Bencoolen and a few other unimportant places in Sumatra. These three points were all acquired primarily for the purposes of trade, although the strategic factor was also operative in the acquisition of Singapore. There was also the spur of colonial rivalry. If we had not acquired them, the Dutch or the French would have done so.

It was because the needs of trade would not permit of chaotic conditions in the interior that the four Malay states of Perak, Selangor, Pahang, and Negri Sembilan (the last an assemblage of nine small states) came under British protection during the last century. They formed the second category, the Federated Malay States. Take the case of Perak, for example. In 1818 the Siamese conquered Perak. In 1824 its independence was guaranteed by a treaty between Siam and Great Britain. For fifty years it was ruled by its own sultans. In 1874, owing to internal strife, the sultan appealed for British protection and the Governor of the Straits

C

Settlements sent a British Resident to Perak. But the Resident was murdered, a punitive expedition became necessary, the murderers were hanged, and the state passed under British administration. The same thing happened in the case of Selangor, which at the beginning of the last century was under Dutch control. The first political contact with the British took place in 1818, when a commercial treaty was signed with the Governor of Penang. From 1867 to 1873 there was acute civil war in the state. An act of piracy off the coast, directed at a British ship, led to British intervention. As a result of disturbances in Negri Sembilan in 1873 a small force was sent to restore order. In 1886 these states also came under British protection. In the case of Pahang on the east coast, a treaty was signed in 1887 with the sultan, who agreed to accept a consular agent to look after the interests of British nationals engaged in trade. Shortly afterwards a British national of Chinese race was murdered, there were disturbances for several years, and eventually, in 1894, we sent a small military expedition and took over the administration.

In the third category were the Unfederated Malay States— Kedah, Perlis, Kelantan, and Trengganu in the north, and Johore in the south. The first four passed under British protection as late as 1909, when Siam ceded her sovereign rights over them in return for the abolition of British extraterritorial rights in Siam, and also, I believe, for some large British railway loan. For several years these states had been administered by British officials in the service of the Siamese Government, and the change-over was effected without any disturbances. (In their propaganda after the outbreak of war the Thais began to revive their claims on these four states. Some people thought that they were possibly part of the bait whereby Japan secured, firstly, Thai acquiescence, and later, active Thai co-operation. It looks, however, as if the Thais are going to be disappointed.)

Relations with the state of Johore, the most southerly state on the mainland, were close throughout the last century, but the formal treaty with the Sultan was only signed in 1914. It is worth noting that there were large Japanese holdings in Johore. Deriving as he did a large proportion of his income from Japanese sources, the Sultan was always disposed to keep in well with the

Japanese. He himself was anti-British, the result of hurt pride. A month after the war started an extensive fifth-column movement was unearthed by our police in Johore and there were several rather abrupt resignations by Malay members of the Johore administration. (Two months after Singapore fell the Sultan was reported by Tokyo radio as having presided at a meeting in Singapore of the Malay sultans convened to discuss measures of co-operation with the Japanese authorities.)

I have touched on this historical aspect of the British administration of Malaya because it should dispel the myth sometimes advanced that the bold, bad British imperialists simply went and seized Malaya at the point of a gun. We did not conquer, we bought, our original footholds. Extension of British influence was gradual. If we had wanted to conquer the peninsula, we could have done so at any time during the last century. As long as our commercial interests were not interfered with, we had no desire to interfere with the internal workings of the Malay states.

Malayan history, before the advent of the British, was a long record of warfare and conflict between petty potentates. The British administration gave to the peninsula nearly a century of peace. As a result of the settled conditions which had prevailed in Malaya throughout the lifetimes of its present inhabitants, war was a phenomenon that was utterly strange to them. Not only war, but even conflict, was something new.

The fact that Malaya had never been fought for had an effect on the British as well as on the natives. The acquisition and retention for over a century of one of the richest colonial areas in the world cost probably less than one hundred British lives. It played an unconscious part in forming the attitude of the British towards Malaya. There was never an army of occupation, although a small garrison was maintained at Singapore. There was never a military governor. Peace was maintained amongst several million people by a civilian police force employing less than two hundred British officers. Although this was a not inconsiderable achievement, it meant also that we never regarded Singapore or Malaya, in the way that we had regarded Gibraltar and Malta, as strategic areas which had been seized by force of arms and had to be retained by force of arms.

The Factual Background

Malaya had a polyglot population. The Japanese never met any national resistance. Of the native sections of the population the Chinese put up the firmest front against the Japanese, some of them inspired by Free China's struggle for survival, others by Soviet precept and example. The Malays, who had had the longest association with the country, took the least interest in the conflict. The peninsula was a battleground for two powers, each of which was fighting far from its bases.

The British civilians in Malaya fell into two main categories. There were the officials. Amongst them were not only the men of the Malayan civil service, but also forest officers, civil engineers, doctors, surveyors, educators, police officers, harbour-masters, and the like. Secondly, there were the men of commerce, the great majority of whom were connected either directly or indirectly with the rubber and tin industries.

Life for the official classes was pleasant and easy-going. The men were well paid and lived in comfortable houses. Most of the routine work was done by competent Eurasian and native clerks who knew the routine far better than their chiefs. The relaxations of the club, a beautiful climate, and a lovely landscape, an adequate salary and regular leave, good communications, a status unchallenged by native aspirations, work that was interesting and rarely strenuous—these things made life in Malaya very pleasant for the official classes. They made life for the commercial classes pleasant also. But the commercial classes never had the same degree of security which the officials enjoyed. Fluctuations in the rubber and tin markets were liable to hit them hard. Many planters were thrown out of work during the depressions. The profits from the rubber and the tin found their way chiefly into the pockets of shareholders in England, not into the pockets of the planters and the mining engineers. The planters, who were nearly always managers of estates owned by joint-stock companies, struck me as being a body of fairly hard-working men, usually adequately but by no means extravagantly paid. I came across a few cases of the 'whisky-swilling planter', but on the whole this is a fiction invented by those who have never been to Malaya.

I hesitate to make any sweeping generalizations about either of these two communities. If one has met and known many indi-

The Supreme Allied Commanders of the Pacific
General Wavell, Admiral Hart (U.S. Navy), and Lieutenant-
General Brett (U.S. Air Corps

Arrival of the British Far Eastern Fleet
The *Prince of Wales* berths at the Naval Base

Air Vice-Marshal Pulford, Air Officer Commanding in Malaya (*on right*), with visiting members of the Netherlands Air Force

Major-General Gordon Bennett, G.O.C., A.I.F., in Malaya, with Major-General Murray-Lyon

viduals, one realizes the dangers and injustices of easy generalization. But I will venture two generalizations, and one private
theory of my own. First, the charge that of recent years we have
not been exporting our best products to the colonies is, in my
opinion, broadly true. Whether the colonies are no longer attract-
ing the adventurous young, or whether there are fewer adventurous young men than there were, I do not know. Perhaps it is
because there are not the opportunities for quick personal advance-
ment that there were. Promotion in the services in Malaya was
almost entirely by seniority. It was difficult for an ambitious
young man to cut out the lower rungs upon the ladder of fame.
There is nothing so deadening to the development of the human
personality as security.

Secondly, as I have emphasized above, Englishmen who had
spent many of their years in the tropics nearly always seemed to
have lost something. It may have been the climate or it may have
been the security and the way of life, but certainly vigour and
idealism rarely survived the early years.

My private theory is that the arrival of white women in the
tropics has had an adverse effect upon the men. In the old days
both officials and planters had their native mistresses. They were
closer to the people of the country. They begat a brood of Eurasian
children, who, if we had been as sensible as the Dutch have been,
could have formed a strong link between the white and the native
elements in the population. The arrival of the white women coin-
cided with, in fact it was made possible by, modern developments
like motor-cars and railways and electricity and frigidaires and
radios. The white woman has inevitably tried to recreate England,
and usually Surbiton, in the tropics. All these things, in my
opinion, have tended to soften the white man and cut him off
from the life and people of the country.

White women will rise indignantly at the above paragraph and
say that the men would not have taken much interest in the
country anyway. Perhaps they are right. The fact remains that
the few thousand British officials and merchants who made their
living out of Malaya were very out of touch with the people. None
of them looked upon Malaya as their home. The ideal of the
Englishman in Malaya and elsewhere in the colonies has always

been to retire to England, and to spend his last few years on English soil. It is an ideal which arouses sympathy. But in Malaya it meant, when taken in conjunction with other factors, that the British and the Asiatics lived their lives apart. There was never any fusion, or even cementing, of the two groups. British rule and culture, and the small British community, formed no more than a thin and brittle veneer. The government treated the natives of the country as a distant but well-disposed father might treat his children. When the crisis came, most of the natives behaved—like children. Whether the British administration of Malaya will in the future be adjudged a success or a failure, the fact remains that after nearly one hundred years of British rule, direct and indirect, the majority of the Asiatics were not sufficiently interested in a continuation of this rule to take any steps to ensure its continuance.

If one was judging British rule in Malaya *in vacuo*, there would be no criterion. But it could be compared with Dutch rule in the Indies. On the whole I think the Dutch made a much better job of the Indies than we did of Malaya, especially as regards the welfare of the natives. The Dutch, of course, had been in the Indies much longer. They had been there for nearly three and a half centuries, except for a brief interregnum of British rule at the beginning of the last century, when Java was administered by Sir Stamford Raffles, who later founded Singapore. Their roots were deeper than those of the British in Malaya, their association with the country both longer and closer. Their colonial effort had not been dispersed in many quarters of the globe, but had been devoted almost exclusively to this rich area in the south-west Pacific. There had been much intermarriage between the Dutch and the people of the country. The offspring of these mixed marriages were not treated as outcasts but were on a par with the white people. There was no colour bar. People of mixed blood could, and did, rise to the highest positions in the Indies. They formed a bridge between the Dutch on the one hand and the natives on the other. The Dutch in the Indies all spoke Malay, and usually spoke it very fluently. Many of them had made the Indies their homes, lived, worked, and retired there, returning to Holland only two or three times perhaps in their lifetimes. Moreover, life for the Dutch in the Indies had been harder in some respects than life in Malaya had been for the British. It was only comparatively recently that many parts of the Indies became peaceful and settled. The Dutch somehow preserved a large measure of the vigour and spirit of the early pioneers.

But, although the Dutch made a good job of the Indies, they also failed, as the British failed, to organize a national resistance amongst the native people whom they governed. The conclusion would seem to be that a colonial army, largely composed of mercenaries, can never be a match for a national army, especially when the latter enjoys vastly superior equipment. Whatever a country's methods of colonial administration may be, there is only one answer to an enemy possessing a formidable force of bomber and fighter planes. That answer is an even greater number of bomber and fighter planes.

4

UNDERESTIMATING THE ENEMY

The cardinal mistake in war is said to be that of underestimating the enemy. And yet that is what both the British and the Americans did in regard to Japan. The Americans minimized Japan's potentialities even more than did the British. To observers in the Far East during the months leading up to the outbreak of war it seemed that America did not treat the Japanese threat at all seriously, that in the estimation of the majority of Americans Japan was a problem that had to be tackled some time but a problem that could be cleaned up without difficulty. All that was necessary was for the Pacific Fleet to sail out of Pearl Harbour, meet the Japanese fleet, and sink it.

There were four main reasons why we underestimated the capacities of the Japanese. First, the official observers based their estimates of Japan's military, naval, and aerial capacity largely upon Japan's performances in China. The fact that after four and a half years of war Japan was still as far from reaching a decision in China as she had been at the beginning was ascribed primarily to military incompetence when it should have been ascribed to diplomatic incompetence. Japan had fairly effective control of China's coastline (although there were still certain leaks in the coastal blockade). She had occupied all the main cities of China, including the industrial coastal and riverine areas. She had control of nearly all China's railways. She had forced her adversary to rely upon two long overland supply routes, the Burma highway and the Red Road to Russia. She had set up an alternative Chinese Government. She had plastered with bombs every city and town of any consequence in every province of China. But she had failed to break the spirit of resistance of the Chinese people or secure the co-operation of any but a negligible minority. The summer of 1941 found the régime headed by that great figure, General Chiang Kai-shek, being accorded an increasing measure

40

Underestimating the Enemy

both of recognition and of concrete assistance by the democracies. It was not Japanese military weakness or incapacity that created the impasse. There was no city in China which Japan could not have taken if she had been prepared to make the necessary effort. She could have marched to Chungking if she had considered it worth her while. Japan failed to reach a decision in China primarily because her officials and her people failed to solve the problem of their relationships with the Chinese. Japan was also fighting against the size of China and against a people who, disunited for centuries, had at last found a bond to unite all sections, the bond of a common hatred of the invader. Most Western observers simplified what was really a very complex affair. How was it, they asked, that a nation supposed to be a first-class military power had failed after four long years to 'defeat' or 'conquer' a people whose military incompetence was legendary? It could only be because that nation was *not* a first-class military power. They forgot that old maxim of Napoleon's, namely, that in warfare the psychological is to the material as three to one.

On the other hand, during the four and a half years of the China war Japan had ample time and opportunity to train, test, and temper a huge national army with actual experience of warfare in the field. Japanese bombers had four years of target practice on real objectives.

Second of the reasons why we underestimated the strength of Japan was an error which the British made at the beginning of the war against Nazi Germany, that of thinking that the enemy could be brought to his knees by economic pressure. We knew that Japan was economically weak. We took measures to make her still weaker. From economic weakness we inferred military weakness. The truth was that Japan's economic weakness would only have told in a long war. The military leaders, by imposing great restrictions on the civil population, had amassed sufficient supplies of oil, iron, and essential materials to embark upon the hazard of a short-term war with a certain conviction that the hazard was worth taking.

Thirdly, it has always seemed to me that the West tends to oscillate between an exaggerated fear of Japan (as expressed in the hackneyed phrases, 'the yellow peril', 'the menace of Japan',

41

and an equally exaggerated contempt for, and disparagement of, the Japanese. In other words, sheer race prejudice played its part in leading us and especially the Americans to underestimate the Japanese. Battleships, submarines, tanks, aeroplanes, these were inventions of the West. It could not be that the East could learn to use these things as efficiently as the West.

Fourthly, Japan's close association with Nazi Germany had effects which we could only judge after war had actually broken out. Hitler has no love for the Japanese. Germans in China have told me that in their estimation there is only one race that Hitler with his inflamed racial pride despises more than the Japanese, and that is the Jews. One has only to read that astonishing paragraph on the Japanese in *Mein Kampf*:

'If from to-day onwards, the Aryan influence on Japan would cease—and if we suppose that Europe and America would collapse —then the present progress of Japan in science and technique might still last for a short duration; but within a few decades the inspiration would dry up, and native Japanese character would triumph, while the present civilization would become fossilized, and fall back into the sleep from which it was aroused over seventy years ago by the impact of Aryan culture.'

But the association of the two countries was natural since both were out to break the *status quo*. Moreover, by trying to bring Japan into the war, Hitler hoped to make the Americans more nervous in the Pacific and thereby check the rising tide of American help to Great Britain. Japan was able to ask her own price. The price (which we may nevertheless be sure Hitler was reluctant to pay) was increased assistance from German technical advisers, especially in the Japanese aircraft industry. They came from Germany in ever increasing numbers. They showed the Japanese how to build Messerschmitts and Stukas and Heinkels. They showed the Japanese how to build larger and better bombs. There was also traffic in the other direction. More and more Japanese went to Germany. Military observers watched the campaigns against Poland, against Norway, against France, against Britain, against Greece, against Crete, against Russia. For example, the Japanese general who commanded the Japanese forces in Malaya, Lieutenant-General Tomoyuki Yamashita, headed in December 1940 a Japanese military mission that went to Germany and Italy to study the war tactics of the Axis at first hand. The Japanese studied the new technique of war as it had been developed and was now being practised by the world's premier military specialists. They saw the importance of the air arm, the advantages of mechanization, the necessity of co-ordinating the land, sea, and air arms in order to form one striking weapon, the role that could be played by a well-organized fifth column, the possibilities of external and internal propaganda, and so forth. All this knowledge found its way back to Japan, was collated, studied, digested, and much of it eventually used. German influence was to be detected in many features of the Pacific war; in the grandiose sweep and suddenness of Japan's initial moves; in the design of her aircraft and in some of the tactics which they practised; in the design and use of her tanks; in her use of the fifth column; in many of her propaganda devices, including widespread bomphleteering and broadcasts by captured troops.

At the same time it is important not to overestimate the effects of German influence. Japan learnt much from Germany because it was Germany who was the chief innovator in the science of war. She learnt from other countries too. A Japanese bomber shot down at Darwin was found to have certain British, American, and Swiss equipment in addition to German equipment. She even learnt from China. The enveloping tactics which she practised in Malaya with such success were only the tactics which Chinese soldiers habitually used against the invaders of their country. Japan also evolved things for herself, as will be seen later. We should be on the safe side if we attributed more to the *indirect* influence of German precept and example than to the direct influence of Nazi diplomats and agents in Tokyo and Berlin.

The Japanese, contrary to the idea universally held about them, are not a nation of servile imitators. Nor, admittedly, are they a nation of creative originators. They are essentially a nation of *exploiters*. Count Keyserling put it well in his *Travel Diary of a Philosopher*, when he likened the Japanese technique to that used by the wrestler in *judo*, who tries to overcome his opponent, not by exerting his own strength, but by turning his opponent's strength against himself. What makes the Japanese so formidable is their combination of a mastery of western technique with a passionate national *élan* and an outlook that is in many ways feudal if not medieval.

It is a mistake to exaggerate the extent of German influence for another reason. Japan neither is nor was a puppet of Nazi Germany. She is not a subsidiary appendage which, when the parent organism is destroyed, will wither and decline of its own accord. If it is true that Germany was using Japan for selfish reasons of her own, it is equally true that Japan was using Germany for selfish reasons of *her* own. Mutual self-interest, and mutual self-interest alone, underlay the Anti-Comintern Pact and the Tripartite Pact. Japan alone decided at what moment and for what reasons and in what way she would go to war in the Pacific. I mention these things because many people seem to think that all we have to do is to defeat Nazi Germany, and that Japan stands or falls with Nazi Germany. Indeed to laymen in the Far East it appeared to be this idea that Mr. Churchill sold to President Roosevelt when he made his visit to Washington in December 1941. I do not contest, for I am not in a position to judge, the argument that the Allies should concentrate on defeating Germany first. But they make a mistake if they think that there will be no necessity eventually to concentrate on Japan also. It is impossible to say that one nation is a graver menace than the other. It may be desirable to deal with the menaces one at a time. But they are essentially coequal menaces, and together they form one single menace, whole and indivisible.

Before passing on to a description of the campaign, there are two questions which might usefully be touched upon.

First, why did Japan go to war with Britain and America? There were several reasons. Japan could not secure what she had come to regard as her minimum national demands without going to war. Economically she was being driven further and further back into a corner, as much by policies of her own choosing as by pressure exerted by the democracies. The only way she could get out of the corner and escape slow strangulation was by fighting her way out. Fundamentally, Japan went to war because she could not

The Author

A young Gurkha in the jungle

Gurkhas with a mortar in the jungle. Note the excellent cover
—there is no field of fire for riflemen

do anything else. Ten years ago Japanese statesmen might have decided whether their country was to march along the road of peaceful progress and international co-operation or along the alternative route of military conquest. But things had gone so far by 1941 that the only decision left to Japanese statesmen was the date on which they would take the plunge. The basic causes of these modern wars seem to be purely economic. Certainly they were primarily economic in the case of Japan. Economic difficulties engendered (in conjunction with the national temperament and the feudal set-up) exactly the same frustration and explosiveness that developed in Germany, and persuaded millions of otherwise sane human beings to sacrifice themselves passionately on the altars of national gods and follow the priests of such cults with a blind unthinking obedience. For the millions of Japan that God was *Dai Nippon*, whose earthly symbol was the semi-divine Emperor; the sacred texts were the Imperial Rescripts; the priesthood was the military caste. It is strange, but nevertheless inescapable, that such phenomena are tied up with those mundane phenomena of rising birth-rates, closing markets, shortages of raw materials, and the like.

At what time did Japan's leaders decide to take the irrevocable step of making war upon Britain and America? Perhaps we shall not know the answer to this momentous question until the memoirs of Japanese leaders are published many years from now. It is my personal opinion that fairly early on in the Sino-Japanese war, when the Japanese were bumping into third-power interests in China at every turn, the Japanese military and naval leaders decided that a war with the democracies would have to be fought soon. Their inability to reach a solution in China, which in Japan was universally but mistakenly attributed to the aid which the democracies were giving to China, and the progress of the war in Europe, which suggested at first that aggression paid and that the democracies were weak and effete, only confirmed them in this decision. For this reason, after two years of war in China, they decided to rest content with the military stalemate and concentrate everything on building up enough reserves of materials for a war with Britain and America. The issue was (in my opinion) forced by the various economic measures which the democracies took against Japan during 1941. The most powerful sections in the Japanese Government had already decided, before opening those abortive negotiations with the Americans which dragged on through the summer and autumn of 1941, that they were prepared to resort to war. They expected to be obliged to fight it but they thought that it might still be worth their while to try and gain their ends by peaceful methods, using exactly the same sort of blackmail that Hitler so often used, the threat of going to war. If the negotiations fell through, Japan would have lost nothing and indeed would have gained a few more months in which to complete her preparations for war and would also have lulled the democracies into a false sense of security. Those preparations must have been completed in November, the final orders must have been given during the first week of December. And in the meantime little Mr. Saburo Kurusu, Ambassador to Belgium and later to Nazi Germany, married to a charming American woman, flew to Washington to make a final attempt, so it was said, to prevent a breakdown of the negotiations and achieve a peaceful settlement of the differences between Japan and the democracies. Had the decision to attack Pearl Harbour on December 8th already been taken when he left? Was he aware of the decision? Was he the ultimate blind? It will be remembered that Mr. Kurusu and the Japanese Ambassador to Washington, the one-eyed Admiral Nomura, had arranged to have an interview with Mr. Hull on the very day that the attack took place. They had the nerve to keep the appointment. They were twenty minutes late for it. Mr. Hull kept them waiting a similar period. They handed to Mr. Hull the Japanese reply to the American Note of November 26th. The saintly Mr. Hull read it carefully. Then he said, so it is reported, that in all his dealings with Admiral Nomura over a period of months, he, Mr. Hull, had never uttered a word of falsehood. But, as regards the Japanese reply, he declared:

'In all my public life I have never seen a document more crowded with infamous falsehoods and distortions, on a scale so huge that I never imagined until to-day that any government on this planet was capable of uttering them.'

5

THE WAR BEGINS

The war began with a bang.

Maria and I lived on top of the highest building in Singapore, the Cathay Building, which also housed the offices of the Malayan Broadcasting Corporation and the Far Eastern headquarters of the Ministries of Information and Economic Warfare. We had gone to bed early. Suddenly, shortly after four in the morning, the first siren began to wail. Rising and falling, rising and falling, it cut across the stillness of the tropic night like some frightful oath uttered in a polite drawing-room. One after the other the sirens from different parts of the city chimed in until they formed one shrill cacophony. If it was eerie for the white people, what chill fear that sound must have struck into the breasts of hundreds of thousands of poor natives in their ramshackle houses of brick and timber! I leapt out of bed and pulled back the curtain. With complete certainty I knew that it was war. A ring of searchlights from their positions round the island were focused straight up into the air, moving backwards and forwards, trying to spot the planes that had caused the alarm. The black-out was not at all good and all the street lights were burning. Suddenly there were bright flashes and loud explosions in the direction of the docks and the centre of the town. The anti-aircraft guns were firing. From where we watched, there were no planes visible, although we could hear the drone of bombers, that low vibration that one *feels* as much as hears. Then some bombs fell down in the same quarter where the guns had been firing, not many, but they made a deeper rumbling sound quite distinct from the loud report of the guns. Then silence. The drone gradually died away. The searchlights continued their search for the raiders. The lights in the streets still shone brightly. One or two cars with dimmed lights sped through the streets. The voices of air-raid wardens, bustling about their duties, drifted up from

47

below. One by one the searchlights were switched off. A long time later the all-clear sounded.

At that time I was working in the Far Eastern Bureau of the Ministry of Information as deputy director to a really outstanding person, still in his early thirties, Rob Scott, of whom more will be heard later. Shortly after the raid was over Rob called me up and asked me to come down to the office. There I learnt that an hour previously the Army Public Relations Unit had summoned all war correspondents and told them that the Japanese had attempted landings at Kota Bahru. British bombers had attacked the Japanese ships. The Commander-in-Chief, Far East, Sir Robert Brooke-Popham, had been up all night with his staff. The Governor of the Netherlands East Indies was expected to make a speech at six o'clock declaring war on Japan. Reports were coming in of raids on Manila and of a big Japanese assault on Pearl Harbour.

In the still hours of the morning we pored over the wall maps of the Far East as we had done so often before, and debated the whole momentous affair. Two emotions were uppermost in our minds. The first was relief. The hideous uncertainty was over at last. We knew now where we stood. At the same time the fact of war was somehow unreal and difficult to believe. Many of us had long held that war was inevitable. To that extent we were psychologically prepared for it. But the reality was different from the expectation. It felt completely unreal. The second emotion uppermost in our minds was one of gladness that Japan had made this frontal assault upon America, mingled with amazement that she had been imbecile enough to make it. America was now in the war right up to the hilt. There could be no talk now of 'pulling Britain's chestnuts out of the fire', as there surely would have been if Japan had attacked only the British Pacific possessions and left America alone for the time being. The attack on Pearl Harbour meant that America was now unconditionally at war with Japan and also, inevitably, at war with Germany. Isolation would vanish overnight. We all agreed (it seems strange to recall now) that no war could possibly have begun in a more auspicious way.

Morning only confirmed that verdict. The bombs dropped during the night had done no important damage but had fallen in the

Major-General Gordon Bennett,
G.O.C. Australian Imperial Forces in Malaya

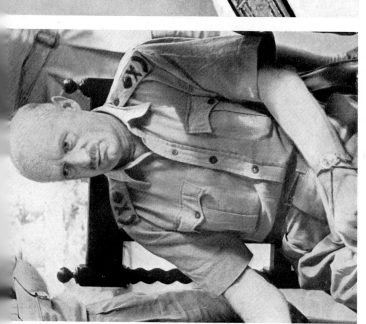

Vice-Admiral Sir Geoffrey Layton,
Commander-in-Chief of the China Squadron,
1939-41

Lieutenant-General Sir L. Heath,
Officer Commanding the British Forces in
North Malaya

Vice-Admiral Sir Tom Phillips (*on the right*),
Commander of the Far Eastern Fleet, with his
Chief of Staff, Admiral Palliser

most conspicuous place in all Singapore, namely, in Raffles Place, in the centre of the main shopping district, where they had demolished half a dozen shops and caused a certain number of casualties, chiefly amongst Sikh watchmen and Chinese shopkeepers. Thousands of people, of all races, went and gaped at this little object lesson in what bombing really meant. That night the blackout was excellent. Two nights later, when we looked down on the city from the watch-tower where we lived, there was hardly a light to be seen. Zealous Chinese volunteers, mostly young men, who formed the backbone of the A.R.P. and all auxiliary services, threw themselves into the task of blacking Singapore out as they might have thrown themselves into some game. The slightest chink of light at a window would provoke frenzied shouts from the street below. Drivers of cars were stopped if their lights were thought to be the smallest degree on the bright side. Anyone attempting to light a cigarette in the street would be fiercely pounced upon from all sides. A few fines were imposed, but the zeal of the Chinese wardens and the desire of the population to comply with the regulations rendered these fines hardly necessary. Singapore's first air raid was not serious enough to cause panic but it served as a spur to galvanize all the civil defence organizations into wartime activity.

The High Command issued three communiqués during the course of the day which revealed that the enemy had effected landings in the Kota Bahru area where confused fighting was taking place, that Japanese landings had also been made at Singora and Patani in south Thailand, and that there had been raids on aerodromes in northern Malaya. The word 'mopping-up' in one of the communiqués led us to assume that the landings were being satisfactorily dealt with. The Governor in a speech to the Legislative Council revealed that there had been 60 fatal casualties in the night's air raid and that 133 people were in hospital. The two Commanders-in-Chief issued a joint Order of the Day which was posted up all over the town in English, Malay, and Chinese. It is worth quoting in full:

'Japan's action to-day gives the signal for the Empire Naval, Army, and Air Forces and for the Forces of the Allies to go into

D

action with a common aim and common ideals. We are ready: we have plenty of warning and our preparations have been made and tested.

'We do not forget at this moment the years of patience and forbearance. We have borne with dignity and discipline the petty insults and insolences inflicted on us by the Japanese in the Far East. We know that those things were only done because Japan thought she could take advantage of our supposed weakness. Now, when Japan herself has decided to put the matter to a sterner test, she will find that she has made a grievous mistake.

'We are confident. Our defences are strong and our weapons efficient. Whatever our race, and whether we are now in our native lands or have come from thousands of miles away, we have one aim and one aim only: it is to defend these shores, to destroy such of our enemies as may set foot on our soil, and then finally to end the power of the enemy to endanger our ideals, our possessions, and our peace.

'What of the enemy? We see before us Japan, drained for years by the exhausting claims of her wanton onslaught on China. We see Japan, whose trade and industry have been so dislocated by these years of reckless adventure that in a mood of desperation her Government have plunged her into war under the delusion that by stabbing a friendly nation in the back she can gain her needs. Let her look at Italy and what has happened since that nation tried a similar base action.

'Let us all remember that we here in the Far East form part of the great campaign for the preservation in the world of truth and justice and freedom. Confidence, resolution, enterprise, and devotion to the cause must and will inspire every one of us in the fighting services, while from the civilian population, Malay, Chinese, or Indian, we expect that patience, endurance, and serenity which is the great virtue of the East, and which will go far to assist the fighting men to gain a final and complete victory.'

Most people in Singapore agreed that it was a pretty good statement, so good that some of them wondered who had written it. It expressed their feelings and gave vent to the confidence which they felt. Meanwhile, many thousands of miles away, another

statement had been promulgated and was being read, by many
perhaps with anxiety, but by all with reverence:

'We, by the grace of Heaven, Emperor of Japan, seated on the
throne of a line unbroken for ages eternal, enjoin upon you, our
loyal and brave subjects: We hereby declare war on the United
States of America and the British Empire. . . .

'The entire nation, with united will, will mobilize its total
strength so that nothing shall miscarry in the attainment of our
aims.

'To ensure the stability of Eastern Asia and to contribute to
world peace is the far-sighted policy which was formulated by our
great, illustrious, Imperial Grandsire and by our great Imperial
Sire succeeding him and which we take constantly to heart. To
cultivate friendship among the nations and to enjoy prosperity in
common with all nations has always been the guiding principle of
our Empire's foreign policy. . . .

'Eager for the realization of their inordinate ambition to dominate the Orient, both America and Britain, in giving support to
the Chungking régime, have aggravated the disturbances in eastern Asia. Moreover, these two Powers, inducing other countries to
follow suit, have increased military preparations on all sides of our
Empire to challenge us. They have obstructed by every means our
peaceful commerce, and finally have resorted to the direct sever-
ance of economic relations, menacing gravely the existence of our
Empire.

'Patiently have we waited and long have we endured in the
hope that our Government might retrieve the situation in peace.
But our adversaries, showing not the least spirit of conciliation,
have unduly delayed a settlement, and in the meantime they have
intensified economic and political pressure to compel our Empire
to submission.

'This trend of affairs would, if left unchecked, not only nullify
our Empire's efforts of many years for the sake of the stabilization
of eastern Asia, but also endanger the very existence of our
nation. The situation being such as it is, our Empire for its existence and self-defence has no other recourse but to appeal to arms
and to crush every obstacle in its path. Hallowed spirits of our

Imperial ancestors guarding us from above, we rely upon the loyalty and courage of our subjects in our confident expectation that the task bequeathed by our forefathers will be carried forward and that the sources of evil will be speedily eradicated and enduring peace immutably established in eastern Asia, preserving thereby the glory of our Empire.'

The day wore on. Little work was done in the office. Everyone was too excited to concentrate on the job in hand. The Malayan Broadcasting Corporation was putting the latest news out at hourly intervals. Each new development was eagerly discussed. The two prevailing emotions, in addition to the general feeling of confidence, were, as I have already pointed out, widespread relief that the uncertainty was over at last, and gladness that the Americans and ourselves were now allies in the field as well as allies in spirit.

There were a few people, however, amongst whom was myself, who had pangs when we thought of some of the implications of the struggle which was now commencing.

In my own case the first two years which I spent in Japan were in many ways the two happiest of my life. Fresh from Cambridge I had gone out to Japan as a professor of English at the Imperial University of Hokkaido in Sapporo. Hokkaido is that remote northern island of the Japanese archipelago, home of the Hairy Ainu, formed largely of snow-covered mountains that provide the best ski-ing in Asia. My duties at the university were arduous but pleasant. I was holding down a job which I felt to be important, teaching large classes of young Japanese, earning my living (at 381 yen a month) for the first time in my life. My relations with the students, with the faculty, indeed with everyone I came into contact with, were as happy as they could be. There was only one other Englishman in Sapporo, the Venerable Archdeacon Batchelor, then some eighty-four years old, 'Father of the Hairy Ainu', compiler of the great Ainu-Japanese-English dictionary, a dear old bearded man with a ninety-three-year-old wife who looked exactly like Queen Victoria, and an adopted Ainu daughter of repellent aspect called Yae. It was the holidays I chiefly loved. My first winter vacation I went over to Peking, where I had been born, and stayed with Colin McDonald, then Peking, now China, correspondent of *The Times*. My first spring vacation, together with an American friend, I made on foot the tour of the eighty-eight temples of Shikoku, the smallest but perhaps the most beautiful of the four main islands of Japan. My first summer vacation I bought two little ponies up in Hokkaido, took them down to the mainland with me, and then rode some six hundred miles on horseback from Morioka to Gotemba, later climbing within the space of ten days the three most famous volcanoes of Japan, Asama-yama, Fuji-san, and Mihara-yama. The next vacation I continued my ride, along the old feudal route from Tokyo to Kyoto, the *Tokaido*, immortalized in the colour prints of Hiroshige and Hokusai. The spring of 1937 I spent in riding round Kyoto and Nara, through the fabled land of Yamato, cradle of the Japanese race, and then returned to Hokkaido and spent a week in bear-hunting up in the mountains with five Ainu hunters and a young Japanese friend. Then, in the summer of 1937, I went over to China and watched the Japanese occupation of Tientsin and the invasion of north China. Returning to Japan I bicycled several hundred miles from Moji to Kyoto, all through the eastern provinces of the main island, and then stayed with my friend John Pilcher in the most beautiful of Japanese houses in Kyoto, most beautiful of Japanese cities. In September I joined the staff of the Embassy as private secretary to Sir Robert Craigie, our newly arrived Ambassador.

There is a sonnet by Wilfrid Scawen Blunt which begins 'He who has once been happy is for aye out of destruction's reach. . . .'

Similarly for the places where we have once been happy, and for the people with whom we have been happy, there is an undertow of sentiment which no subsequent developments can change. The young Japanese doctor who shared my house with me in Sapporo, so good-looking that half the families in the town were trying to secure him as a son-in-law: the young Japanese journalist, an Olympic footballer, with whom I went bear-hunting: young student intellectuals at Sapporo with whom I had argued late into the night; all the friends with whom I had travelled and laughed and drunk and wenched and ridden and gone a-skiing—the memory of these people recurred to me often during the first

The War Begins

few days of the Pacific war. Not that I was sorry the war had begun. Far from it. I was glad that the suspense and uncertainty were over. But it meant that the whole thing was a trifle complicated for me and I was not able to feel the same straightforward simple emotions that seemed to inspire some of my friends.

6

EARLY PERPLEXITIES

There are many puzzles connected with this war in the Pacific which will only be cleared up when the war is over and access is had to all the official documents. The telegrams and dispatches exchanged between the Foreign Office and the British Legation at Bangkok during the weeks preceding, and the hours following, the actual commencement of hostilities ought to make especially interesting reading. Why did we never advance up the Kra Isthmus and prevent the Japanese from landing troops and later consolidating themselves, at Singora and Patani? British troops hung poised on the Thai border and waited for four whole days until they were attacked by the Japanese.

On the evening of December 8th Japanese forces marched into Bangkok after what appeared to have been a few hours of purely token resistance in the morning on the part of the Thai army. The Japanese broadcast an allegation that the British had already advanced into Thailand and that their attack on Thailand was consequent upon the British move. The Foreign Office hotly denied the charge, declared it was wholly untrue, that in no place had any British forces crossed the frontier, when Japan invaded Thailand. But that does not mean that we had no plans made to deny those potential bases on the Kra Isthmus in south Thailand to the Japanese, or that it might not have been wise to take the initiative at once against the enemy. Why did we never move? It could not be because we did not have enough troops since we had all the troops who later fought their way down the west coast. Nor could it be because the attack at Kota Bahru was proving harder than we had expected. The troops in that area were a self-contained body, dependent upon a long and difficult line of communication, half road, half railway. They could not be quickly reinforced. Was it a lack, on the British side, of that 'offensive spirit', about which so much has been written? Was it that the

Japanese in those first attacks on our northern airfields had already destroyed so many of our planes on the ground that, in the air, we were already on the defensive? Or was it that Sir Josiah Crosby was holding out to the British Government the hope of the Thais resisting the Japanese, or at least remaining neutral, if absolutely no provocation was offered them? The last is the most plausible explanation. The answers to these questions will only be answered after the war. They are asked now in no carping or condemnatory spirit. Reasons of weight doubtless kept our troops in in Kedah immobilized during the first days of the campaign, those days which are so tremendously important in any campaign. But the fact remains that the Japanese early in the campaign achieved advantages whose true import only became apparent very much later. They not only took, but retained, the initiative, and put us on the defensive. The great lesson of modern warfare, perhaps of all warfare, is—Attack! Attack! and again Attack! To have the initiative is to have another ally fighting with you. Besides, the terrain in Malaya, contrary to what some of our experts thought, was infinitely more adapted to offence than to defence. It offered perfect cover to an attacking force. It was all very well to have your defence outposts out in the jungle. Often they could not see more than fifty yards in any direction. Thus it was easy for enemy troops to infiltrate between these posts without being seen, let alone attacked, and then to reassemble behind our lines. Failing to secure the initiative during the opening stages of the campaign, we never afterwards recaptured it, and the Japanese gained, in Singora and Patani, two excellent rear bases from which to fight a campaign down the Malayan peninsula. Without such bases they could not have fought any campaign at all. Only later did we appreciate what a precious thing the initiative could be, when we saw the effect on tired troops of weeks of defensive fighting and steady withdrawal, during which time they had never once possessed the initiative themselves. Similarly it was only later that we realized the true implications of the contents of the communiqué which was published on December 9th. It was a longish document.

'The Japanese', it said, 'had been using large numbers of aero-

planes in an endeavour to gain a measure of air superiority in
northern Malaya, so as to cover their landings in southern Thailand and their continued efforts to gain control of the Kota Bahru
aerodrome in Kelantan. Air reconnaissance yesterday established
that twenty-five further transports were proceeding down the
coast of southern Thailand escorted by warships, apparently preparing to land additional troops in the Singora, Patani, and Kota
Bahru areas. Thus all the transports that were located in the air
reconnaissance of December 6th and 7th are now apparently engaged in these landings in the Kra Isthmus and in north-east
Malaya. . . .

'Fighting in the Kota Bahru area has been severe, and
although by noon yesterday a large measure of control had been
achieved by our forces in this area, further landings took place in
the afternoon, and heavy fighting for control of the aerodrome
took place last evening and continued throughout the night. The
situation in this area is still confused, but reinforcements should
reach there during the day. . . .

'It is as yet too early to attempt to forecast what the Japanese
main plan is; but there are indications that, following the collapse
of resistance in Thailand and the heavy scale of his air effort from
his bases in Indo-China, he is prepared to engage considerable
forces in an endeavour to obtain control of northern Malaya. This
move was always foreseen to be a likely one, and the disposition of
our forces was designed to meet it.'

We did not know down at Singapore (nor, to do them justice,
did the High Command) what was really going on in north-east
Malaya. Only the barest of operational reports were coming
through. It was only many days later that we learned from men
who had been there the details which could have made those staid
sentences in the communiqué throb with life. The enemy was in
truth 'endeavouring to gain a measure of air superiority'. Formation after formation of twin-engined bombers was raiding our
northern airfields, bombing with remarkable accuracy, dropping
stick after stick of bombs across hangars and installations, destroying many of our precious bombers and fighters on the ground. On
the beaches south of Kota Bahru the Japanese had landed from

transports anchored some distance off-shore, making use of the same shallow metal barges that they had used in their landing operations on the China coast. A withering fire met them. Our bombers flew over, dropped bombs on the transports, machine-gunned the barges. Japanese losses must have been very heavy indeed. Nothing daunted, they came on. The barges were run up on the shore. Men leapt from them and made up the beach. Less than half would reach the fringe of trees, but these would ensconce themselves as best they could. More and more came on. Those who had reached the jungle and taken up positions in the rear and to the flank of our positions on the beaches eventually made those positions untenable. Our forces withdrew inland, leaving behind them hundreds of corpses being washed in the surf or stiff and crumpled on the sand. From then on it was jungle fighting of a type that will be described in detail in a later chapter. But we had no idea of these things down in Singapore. The news was not good, admittedly. It might be better. But surely it ought to be possible to mop those Japanese up without much difficulty. Certainly there were no grounds yet for pessimism or despondency.

7

THE FIRST BIG BLOW

The *Prince of Wales* and the *Repulse* arrived in Singapore on December 2nd. In command of the new British Far Eastern Fleet, which was to take the place of the old China Squadron, was Vice-Admiral Sir Tom Phillips, previously Vice-Chief of the Naval Staff. I have already described the enthusiasm and confidence which its arrival occasioned. Singapore's significance was no longer largely potential. It was actual. It was real. It was a dream come true.

Again there is a mystery which will only be cleared up after the war. What passed at those fateful secret conferences held on Monday, December 8th, when the future moves of the battleships were discussed and decided? Did the commander of our air forces in Malaya tell the naval chiefs that he was not in a position to supply land-based aircraft for the protection of the big ships supposing they were attacked from the air? Did Admiral Phillips, itching to attack the enemy, feel that the risk of proceeding northward without adequate air protection to harry Japanese transports in the Gulf of Siam was a justifiable risk? Or did he feel that, as his ships were certain to be bombed if they remained anchored in the Straits of Johore, it was preferable to run the risk of being bombed when taking part in offensive action against the enemy? For the present one can only speculate on the answers to these questions.

Certainly we knew in Singapore on the Tuesday morning that the ships had sailed. And about four the following afternoon the incredible news was first bruited around that they had been sunk by Japanese aircraft. Official confirmation was contained in the B.B.C. news that evening, and at eight-thirty Mr. Duff Cooper made a broadcast over the Singapore radio.

I still remember the chill sense of calamity which was caused by the loss of these two ships. It was worse than calamity. It was calamity that had the premonition of further calamity. No details were available that evening although most people had visions of Japanese suicide squads flying their loaded planes straight into the ships. For the first time we had an inkling of what the true balance of factors was in this Pacific war. We saw before us, still vaguely perhaps, that long dark tunnel through which we should have to pass before we emerged in the sunlight on the far side. Blown clean away at one fell swoop was one of the main pillars on which our sense of security rested. Nor was our despondency in any way mitigated by Mr. Duff Cooper's Churchillian heroics and his well-intentioned attempt to reconcile people in Singapore to the news. This was not the first time in their long history of glory, he said, that the British peoples had met with disaster and surmounted it. Britain had other battleships and was building others yet. Malaya stood now only where she stood a month ago. 'We were not safe then: we are not safe now. But in these great days, safety seems hardly honourable and danger is glorious.' The argument that we were only where we had been a month ago was one that struck most people as being ingenious rather than sound. The *Prince of Wales* and the *Repulse* were lost. That was all we knew, all we could think of.

Early the following morning it was announced that out of the 2,923 men aboard the two ships over 2,330 had been rescued. Most of them were already in Singapore. Two correspondents who had been on the *Repulse*, O. D. Gallagher of the *Daily Express*, and Cecil Brown of C.B.S. (the Cassandra already referred to), were even now hammering out their stories in the Press office attached to the Combined Services Public Relations Unit. Both looked worn and unshaven, Gallagher suffering still from giddiness caused by getting oil into his system as he was floundering about in the water.

Gradually one was able to piece the story together. As the fleet headed north up the Malayan coast on the evening of Monday, December 9th, Admiral Phillips signalled from the *Prince of Wales*:

'We are looking out for trouble. No doubt we shall find it. We hope to surprise enemy transports to-morrow and expect to meet the Japanese battleship *Kongo*. I am sure every man will give a good account of himself.'

As darkness fell a Japanese reconnaissance plane approached at a great height and then made off. Actually Japanese reconnaissance planes flying over Singapore on Tuesday, when they had twice caused the alarm to be sounded, had already discovered that the fleet had sailed from Singapore. Japanese reports later claimed that Japanese submarines operating off the coast of Malaya had also observed the fleet on Tuesday when it was heading north.

The Admiral, knowing that his fleet had been spotted, changed course during the night. However, it was picked up by reconnaissance planes the following morning and, according to my information, the fleet turned round and began to head south.

At eleven o'clock a formation of bombers was seen approaching at a height of 15,000 feet and the order 'Action Stations' was given. The bombers, with phenomenal accuracy, scored hits on both ships. One bomb pierced the aircraft hangar of the *Repulse*, penetrated to the marines' mess deck, and started a fire which was still burning when the ship went down.

Shortly after this attack, torpedo-carrying aircraft appeared on the scene. An official naval photographer described to me how they came skimming low over the water at a height of only twenty feet, dropped their torpedoes at a distance of some four hundred yards and then pulled up and away. They attacked from all sides. The anti-aircraft guns on the two battleships, which were capable, especially at short range, of putting up a pretty considerable barrage, blazed furiously and sent seven of the attackers crashing into the sea. But the attacks were pressed relentlessly home, the Japanese showing, it must be admitted, considerable skill and daring. The *Prince of Wales* was hit and her stern damaged. She signalled to ask the *Repulse* if she had been hit. The *Repulse* replied:

'Have avoided nineteen torpedoes till now, thanks to Providence.'

The first wave of torpedo-carrying aircraft drew off. Hardly had they gone when there was another high-level bombing attack by a formation of Japanese bombers but this time they failed to secure any hits although bombs fell all round the battleships.

Then more waves of torpedo-carrying planes attacked. The *Repulse* was hit on her bow, on her port beam, on her stern. She began to settle. The captain ordered all hands to abandon ship. The ship heeled slowly over until she lay at an angle of forty-five degrees. It was not possible to launch any of the boats. Men began to slither down the ship's sides and jump into the sea which was covered with a thick scum of fuel oil. They swam as best they could in the thick oil or clung to rafts and pieces of wreckage or floated with the aid of lifebelts. The sea was covered with bobbing heads. Japanese planes circled round overhead but made no attempt to machine-gun the survivors in the water. Then at twelve-thirty the *Repulse* threw her bows up into the air and disappeared under the surface of the ocean, leaving a placid, heaving oily swell, broken only by the bobbing heads of men struggling in the water. A few miles away the *Prince of Wales* could be seen belching forth smoke. Then she too went under, at about one o'clock. Fortunately the two escorting destroyers were not attacked at all during this engagement and at once they set about the task of picking up as many survivors from the sea as they could. There is a story, never officially reported or confirmed, that, after the two battleships had been sunk, the Japanese aeroplanes signalled to the destroyers that they could set about the task of rescuing survivors without fear of molestation. There is so little chivalry and gallantry about modern warfare that one would like to be able to believe this story, but it is probably apocryphal.

An official communiqué later revealed that 'within one hour of news of the attack reaching an aerodrome 160 miles distant our fighters were on the scene but by that time the enemy planes had withdrawn.'

Admiral Phillips and Captain Leach of the *Prince of Wales* both went down in the flagship, although Captain Tennant of the *Repulse* was rescued. For several days afterwards survivors from the two ships were to be seen in the streets of Singapore, wearing whatever clothes and uniforms they had been able to find, some of them heavily bandaged where they had been burned or injured. A few of them later played a part in the defence of Singapore Island.

The loss of these two ships had widespread effects.

The sinking of the two main units of the British Far Eastern Fleet, in conjunction with the elimination for the time being of the American Pacific Fleet at Pearl Harbour, gave the Japanese a temporary naval control in the south-west Pacific that was almost unchallenged, and altered the whole balance of naval power in the Pacific in their favour. The premises on which Singapore's defence rested no longer existed. Thenceforward Japan's long ocean lines of communication, which were one of her most vulnerable points, were never seriously menaced. (Japan incidentally missed a big opportunity during the days immediately following these two victorious sallies against the fleets of the democracies. If she had amassed her naval strength in the Pacific and sailed resolutely eastward, nothing on earth could have prevented her from shelling the Panama Canal and posssibly putting it out of action for the rest of the war.)

The news of the sinkings had wide repercussions throughout the world. I suspect there were many sections of Japanese opinion who did not greet the declaration of war on Britain and America with any but the gloomiest apprehension. Many Japanese felt that war with the democracies was tantamount to racial suicide. To defeat America Japan would have to invade America, which she could never do. Whatever the then balance of material resources might be, there was no doubt whose were the greater *potential* resources. In other words Japan was embarking upon a war which she could not possibly win, and which she could very possibly lose. Moreover there was a very genuine war-weariness prevalent in Japan when the war started. The 'Incident' had dragged on for four and a half weary years, involving increasing deprivations for the Japanese people. It still showed no signs of coming to an end. The United States, to many Japanese, represented the zenith of that technological civilization to which they had always aspired. American prestige was high, as it is still high throughout the Far East, without the Americans having to resort to deliberate attempts to boost their prestige. But there is nothing in this world that succeeds like success. The effect of these early successes was to unite the Japanese people behind their government and to transform the war from a desperate act of self-preservation, disguised for propaganda purposes as a crusade to liberate millions of groaning Asiatics from the shackles of white imperialists, into the most triumphant smash-and-grab raid in history. Looting (whatever moral views we may hold on it) is a pastime as delicious to a nation as to a soldier. In the same way, Hitler's victories during the first year of war in Europe popularized the war and united the German people still further behind the war effort.

These successes also had an effect on Japan's neighbours who were trying to sit on the fence. Thailand soon afterwards announced a sweeping programme of co-operation with Japan. They dampened the spirits of our allies, the Chinese, who had greeted the outbreak of war in the Pacific with tremendous enthusiasm, feeling that at last they had secured active allies in the struggle which they, a pacific and unmilitary people, had been fighting so gallantly for four and a half years. And in Malaya the loss of these two great ships, whose arrival in Singapore had been the occasion of so much publicity, acted as dynamite to the complacency of the British, who perceived clearly many, if not all, of the implications of this sudden disaster.

Australian troops digging trenches in a rubber plantation on Singapore island. The intervals between the trees are wide enough for the passage of a tank

A Tamil with his family takes refuge in the jungle

Long grass in the jungle—another example of the cover for attacking troops

Colonel Ian Stewart,
O.C. Argyll and Sutherland Highlanders

8

THE BATTLE OF KEDAH

While tragedy was being enacted off the Malayan coast, big things were happening on the mainland.

But first of all there is another little Malayan mystery that I should like to refer to. Early on the morning of December 10th the Japanese were reported to have attempted a landing on the east coast at Kuantan, where, according to the communiqué, they were being engaged by our troops and attacked by our aircraft. Kuantan was a small port on the east coast some two hundred miles from Singapore where an airfield had recently been constructed. There was no road along the coast north or south but a road ran inland in the direction of Kuala Lumpur. The next communiqué said that there had been 'no report of further attempts to land in the Kuantan area', the next but one that 'there is no change in the Kuantan area'. References to Kuantan continued for several days.

The funny thing is that no Japanese forces ever landed at Kuantan, nor to the best of my knowledge, ever attempted to do so. When Kuantan was eventually attacked, it was attacked by a Japanese force that made its way overland all the way down the coast from Kota Bahru. I never discovered what the true explanation was. There must have been some sort of false alarm at Kuantan one night and this gave rise to the belief that landings had been attempted here. Goats, wandering on the beaches, sometimes touched off the land-mines. A goat may well have been responsible for the paragraphs of description and speculation which newspapermen began to send about 'the Kuantan front'.

About this time I joined the ranks of the newspapermen myself. *The Times*, finding themselves without a war correspondent in Malaya, cabled asking if they could nominate me immediately to the post of war correspondent in Malaya. Their string man was David Waite, the able young editor of the *Singapore Free Press*,

E

but David Waite was tied to Singapore and was not able to make trips up-country. Rob Scott, when I showed him the telegram, agreed to release me at once from the Ministry of Information, with an alacrity that sprang, I think, largely from his own desire to go and watch the war instead of toiling in the office routine at Singapore.

Early on the morning of December 12th the Japanese launched a fierce attack on our positions on the Thai border in Kedah. (For four whole days, therefore, our troops had sat up there on the frontier doing nothing while the Japanese poured men and equipment into Singora and Patani less than one hundred miles north. Our men expected the order to advance. But they waited for it in vain. It never came.) Fighting went on all day. The situation was reported as 'confused', how confused we only learned several days later when we heard what the fighting up on the frontier had been like. It went very badly indeed for us. The Japanese attacked our positions in considerable force; nearly all were armed with tommy-guns, they used armoured vehicles which we had not been expecting; they dressed up as Malays and penetrated our lines; they surrounded our outposts in the jungle and shot them up from all sides; they produced pretty fair disorganization and confusion.

Although little of this was filtering down to Singapore, it soon became evident that the Japanese were advancing, and advancing pretty quickly. In my first dispatch to *The Times*, sent on December 14th, I said:

'Fighting continues in the Kedah area, which is still the main theatre of operations in the Malayan peninsula. Japanese forces, including mechanized units strongly supported by aircraft, have crossed by road from Singora on the Thai coast, and are now seeking to press down the coastal plain of Kedah to Penang.

'Although the backbone of the peninsula at this point is thickly covered with jungle, a wide strip along the coast is composed of rice-fields, and farther inland there is undulating country, devoted mostly to rubber plantations. On both of these two types of terrain mechanized units would have no difficulty in operating. The country on the west coast of Malaya is much easier and communications more developed than on the jungle-covered east coast. In certain areas our forces, mainly British and Indian troops, have been forced to new positions. Fresh reinforcements, both of infantry and aircraft, have been sent north in an effort to stabilize the line.

'There is no disposition here to minimize the threat that may develop to Penang if the present Japanese advance is not stemmed.'

The next day I cabled:

'Further withdrawals took place to-day in the Kedah area, and our troops are still falling back upon prepared positions. R.A.F. fighters have been active in north Malaya and have harried enemy reinforcements coming south from Singora. More than six hundred European men, women, and children, evacuated from Penang, reached Singapore by rail this morning, and others are expected soon.

'While there have been no further developments in Kelantan and Kuantan, there have been signs of further enemy activity. The situation is considered to have many dangerous possibilities and some commentaries from London and elsewhere appear to observers in Singapore to take an over-optimistic view of the situation. The enemy has already shown that he is relying much upon the suddenness and surprise of his attack, and there are still strategic points in Malaya at which he might strike.'

(I do not know where I obtained the information about R.A.F. fighters 'harrying' enemy reinforcements. It was almost certainly untrue. The last sentence was an attempt to get past the censor a warning to readers in London that they must not be surprised if an attack were made in force upon the Malayan coast, or even upon the island of Singapore. Many more transports were reported to have been seen steaming south through the Gulf of Siam.)

Caution was amply justified, for within three days the Japanese had occupied Penang.

This island off the west coast of Malaya, second only to Singapore in the volume of its trade, suffered some of the worst air raids of the whole campaign. Only at Penang did the Japanese make deliberate and sustained attacks upon the civilian population, chiefly Asiatic. Thereafter they confined themselves, with occasional lapses, to military objectives.

The first major raid took place early on the morning of December 11th, when twenty-seven Japanese bombers flew over the island in perfect V-formation. Instead of taking shelter, tens of thousands of people stood in the streets and open places and watched this strange sight in the sky. The bombers flew over the town, and then wheeled back, and in groups of three dive-bombed the town. Wave after wave of them went into shallow dives, dropped their bombs, pulled up, circled around, and then came back again. Some of their bombs were heavy demolition bombs; some were the light anti-personnel bombs, with no penetrating power, some were incendiary bombs of the type that scatter hundreds of pieces of some substance like red sealing-wax, the smallest piece of which can start a fire if it lands on some inflammable material. Nearly all the bombs were dropped on the densely crowded native quarters in Georgetown. When they had unloaded their cargoes, the planes came back and cruised up and down the main streets machine-gunning people in the streets. This went on for nearly two hours. Many fires were started and there were hundreds of casualties.

There was unutterable confusion. All the essential services broke down. The first reaction of the native population was to make a beeline for the hills on the mainland. The auxiliary services, manned chiefly by young Chinese, did what they could. But it was the first job they had tackled. A direct hit on the fire-station meant that there were no fire-engines to put out the fires. Fires went on burning for days. There was no labour to help clear away the dead. Corpses lay on the sidewalks under the burning sun and soon began to smell to high heaven. Rats and pariah dogs sneaked round the corpses. Men who had been in Penang at the time told me that the stink of rotting flesh was something appalling. Shopkeepers boarded up their shops and made for the mainland with what chattels they could take. Looting began almost at once. Many of the native constables of the police disappeared and it was difficult to enforce order. Gangs of Tamils and Chinese roamed the streets, breaking into any building where they thought they might find something of value. There was no labour to man the ferries, no labour to fight the fires, no labour to search for victims buried beneath the ruins of demolished buildings, no labour to clear away the debris, no labour to remove the night-soil, no labour to clear away the rotting and putrescent dead. Labour evaporated into the hills on the mainland.

Exactly the same thing happened on the following day. On the third day, December 13th, Japanese bombers appeared, but for the first time they met with some opposition from British fighters based on the airfield at Butterworth on the mainland. On the evening of that day the process of evacuating all British nationals began. It took about two days.

The evacuation of Penang forms Malayan Mystery No. 4. The order to evacuate Penang, whether it came from the Malayan or the local military command (it certainly did not come from the civil government in Singapore) specified, if my information is correct, that only British nationals of pure British race were to be evacuated. No Asiatics were permitted to evacuate, no Eurasians, and, according to stories widely current in Singapore, not even some Eurasian wives of British nationals. I must make it clear that I do not know the true facts leading up to the evacuation of Penang. But I do know what effects the evacuation had on native morale throughout Malaya. They were calamitous. The British, so it was universally held amongst Asiatics, had ratted out of Penang, had thought of saving no skins but their own, and left the Asiatics to their fate at the hands of the Japanese as if they didn't give a damn what happened to them, had not even told the Asiatics that they were leaving but had suddenly legged it as hard as they could. I do know that three senior members of the Malayan Civil Service felt the disgrace so deeply that, after Penang had actually been occupied by the Japanese, they petitioned the Governor to be allowed to proceed to Penang as an act of restitution to the native populace. Only one Britisher insisted upon staying at Penang, Dr. Evans, of the General Hospital. I believe that he was allowed by the Japanese to carry on with his work. The Ceylonese editor of the *Straits Echo*, Mr. Savaranamuthu, a lawyer who had studied at Cambridge, continued to bring out his paper right until the very end, even when it was simply a broadsheet produced on a hand-press turned by himself. (The Japanese appointed this man Chief of a Peace Preservation Council which they set up in Penang and later made him Commissioner for the Federated Malay States. Mr. Chrysostom, representative of the *Straits Echo* in Singapore, used to assure me most warmly that his chief was quite incapable of becoming a quisling, but appearances are against him. Of Savaranamuthu's courage during the days that led up to the Japanese occupation, however, there can be no doubt.)

Again, I do not know how far the charges are true that the scorched-earth policy was but feebly implemented at Penang. I do know, however, that the Penang radio station was left untouched. One would think that a radio station would be not only one of the first objectives to deny to the enemy but also that it would be such an easy thing to destroy. Two minutes with a sledge-hammer and all that delicate machinery would be completely unserviceable. Nevertheless, the day after the Japanese occupied Penang, the Penang radio was on the air, broadcasting on the same wavelength that thousands of listeners on the peninsula were accustomed to (so that many of them continued to listen regularly), but now giving broadcasts whose contents were strange to them. The broadcasts in English would usually begin: 'Hello, Singapore, this is Penang calling; how do you like our bombings?' Broadcasts were given in all the languages of Malaya, including special talks for Indian troops. The latter were somewhat ineffective as no receiving sets were available to the Indian troops. Native residents would be dragged to the microphone to give flattering accounts of Penang under Japanese occupation. Indian clerks in government departments would tell how, whereas formerly they had been junior underlings, now they were heads of their departments. Two items broadcast over the radio (and also disseminated by the very efficient Japanese rumour-spreading organization in Singapore) had a particularly adverse effect upon native morale. The first emphasized that rice was being distributed in Penang at a far cheaper price than prevailed in those parts of Malaya under British control. Secondly, the head in Penang of the United China Relief Fund (the Chungking régime's overseas collecting organization for the remittance of funds to China to help the Chinese war effort) was reported to have been executed in front of his house, in full view of his wives, children, and relatives.

Penang was a major scandal. But the outcry which it provoked was not without some useful results. It brought home to the British officials and residents their sense of responsibility to those native peoples whom they purported to govern and with whom they lived and worked. European and Asiatic were henceforward treated with a much greater degree of equality, and the scorched-earth policy was more rigorously enforced.

9

VISIT TO THE FRONT

At the beginning of the war there were some twenty correspondents at Singapore. Of the British there was Kenneth Selby-Walker, an old friend from China where he had been Reuter's Far Eastern Manager; Gallagher of the *Daily Express*, who left for Burma shortly after his experience in the *Repulse*; Lawrence Impie of the *Daily Mail*, who had filed telegrams to that paper from China for many years. Later arrivals included Ronnie Matthews of the *Daily Herald*. Most of the men working on the Singapore papers were also holding down string jobs for London papers and agencies. There was quite a corps of Australian journalists, evidence of the keen interest which Australia was taking in this northern outpost of her own defence. Harry Standish of the *Sydney Morning Herald*, who used to file both to his own paper and to the *Daily Telegraph*, was my chief competitor, but I never used to think of him as such. Ian Fitchett, the official Australian observer, did a particularly good job of reporting when the Australian forces went into action in Johore. The others included Bill Knox of the *Sydney Mirror*; Tom Fairhall of the *Sydney Telegraph*; Douglas Wilkie of Sir Keith Murdoch's group of papers; Henry Stokes, formerly of Reuter's, now with the Australian Broadcasting Commission; Ray Maley of the Australian Associated Press; Colin Fraser of the *Sun-Pictorial* of Melbourne. The Americans were also well represented. Yates McDaniel of Associated Press, last correspondent out of Singapore, who was bombed and sunk on his way to Sumatra, and Harold Guard of United Press, an Englishman who spent fifteen years in submarines in the British Navy before he took to journalism, both emerged from the war in Malaya with enhanced reputations. Other American correspondents, some of whom were in Singapore when the war started, some arriving later, included Tilman Durdin of the *New York Times*, Al Noderer of the *Chicago Tribune*,

72

Visit to the Front

George Weller of the *Chicago Daily News*, Cecil Brown of the Columbia Broadcasting System, and Martin Argonsky of the National Broadcasting Commission.

Shortly after the war started a small group of correspondents left for the front with a British conducting officer. Four staff cars, an army truck, and a dispatch-rider, were placed at the disposal of the Public Relations unit. The programme was usually as follows. The correspondents and their conducting officer would make their rear headquarters some forty or fifty miles behind the front. The day would be devoted to a tour of the forward areas, calling in at the various headquarters—corps, division, brigade, battalion, or company—chasing whatever good stories there might be, and then in the evening hammering out the various dispatches at rear headquarters. The dispatches would then be sent down to Singapore either by rail or by dispatch-rider to be censored and telegraphed. There were usually between four and twelve correspondents up-country, some, like myself, preferring to spend most of our time in this way rather than down in Singapore where news of the fighting was always two days old. Visits to Singapore were necessary both to pilot our stories through the censorship and to keep in touch with developments down there. Rear headquarters was usually some large house in a beautiful garden, belonging to an official or a rubber planter, who had already evacuated southwards. Within a zone fifty miles behind the front line there were always many empty houses. They were freely used both by ourselves and by the armed forces. The officer who throughout the campaign did nearly all the conducting was a young British captain, of great enterprise and incredible vitality, called Henry Steel. The correspondents owe him a lasting debt. No risk was too great for him; he was extremely efficient; and he established excellent relations with the officers whom we used to interview.

Being a war correspondent in Malaya was an arduous but not particularly heroic business. Dashing about as we did in staff cars up near the front, we were an obvious target for any Japanese dive-bombers which might be flying round. Often these dive-bombers, operating usually in groups of three, would bomb the roads and machine-gun any transport they could find. Our staff cars were not only somewhat conspicuous targets but also had no aperture in the roof through which a man could stand and spot planes. We would cruise along, therefore, with our eyes to the windows trying to spot any approaching plane as best we as could. Suddenly a man would cry, 'Three planes coming'. Quickly the driver would stop the car and pull under any cover that was available. The occupants would jump out and take cover quickly. Usually we found ourselves in one of the rubber plantations that flank many of the main roads on the west coast. They provide fairly good cover from the air. We would lie on our bellies hoping that the planes would make off. There are few sensations so unpleasant as to lie on your belly in a rubber plantation while Japanese bombers circle around overhead, their attention caught by some suspicious movement on the ground. There is perhaps one more unpleasant sensation—and that is to lie on your belly in open country without even the concealment offered by rubber trees. Eventually the noise would draw off, we would emerge from our hiding-places, and the journey would be resumed. Bombs were aimed at the cars on more than one occasion but none was ever hit (except during a raid at Singapore when the truck was hit and became a total loss) nor were there any casualties amongst the correspondents throughout the Malayan campaign. Rarely did we penetrate into the firing line, for the simple reason that, up at the front, there was the constant danger of being cut off. Henry Steel would sometimes take one correspondent right up forward on the pillion of a motor-bicycle, but one rarely saw any action and most of the correspondents covered the Malayan war without ever once seeing the opposing infantry. There was never a 'front' on the mainland. There were only forward outposts out in the jungle. Only once during the whole campaign was there a front and that was during the few days that the opposing British and Japanese forces first looked at each other with field-glasses and then fired at each other with field-guns across the Straits of Johore.

Shortly after I joined the ranks of the correspondents I made my first visit up-country. I found that I was getting very poor material in Singapore, most of it second-hand, and I was anxious to see the war for myself. P.R. rear headquarters was then in Kuala Lumpur, the main city on the mainland and capital of the Federated Malay States.

Visit to the Front

The trip was not particularly eventful as far as personal adventures were concerned. But it was exceedingly interesting and enabled me to form a picture of what the fighting was like. The most northerly point we reached was Taiping, a town some fifty miles south of Penang. Its airfield was twice bombed during the couple of hours we were there. For the first time since China I saw Japanese bombers zooming down, watched the curious curve which the falling bombs make, listened to the shattering explosion. The enemy planes were completely unopposed.

I learned also how heavy had been the initial fighting at Jitra on the Thai border. The Japanese assault had been delivered with tremendous impetus and had caused great disorganization. Battalions became separated, A company lost touch with B company. Small sections found themselves cut off in the jungle without any idea of what had happened to the rest of their unit. Many of the men we met on that first trip to the front had been completely cut off in that initial fighting but somehow had succeeded in making their way south and rejoining their units. At first it was thought that our casualties had been very heavy. But more and more men kept on turning up. The following story of three sepoys of the Dogra Regiment was typical of many. Cut off from their main unit at Alor Star, they made their way across country to the west coast and came out at Prai, near Penang. Here some friendly Malays gave them food, sarongs, and a small boat. They set off down the coast. But a Japanese patrol boat became suspicious, fired at them, and forced them to land. In another coastal village some Indians gave them loincloths and they shed their sarongs. They thought that they would have a better chance of making their way south dressed as Indians rather than as Malays. They then walked down the coast to Port Weld and finally rejoined their unit at Kuala Kangsar, having walked nearly two hundred miles in one week. They fed chiefly on bananas, papayas, mangosteens, and other tropical fruit which they found by the wayside.

A colonel and major of the Gurkhas, cut off near Alor Star, travelled south about eighty miles parallel with the Japanese advance. They also safely rejoined their unit.

Two officers and twelve men of the East Surrey Regiment, cut off near Jitra on the border, also made their way westwards to the coast. They spent the first two nights in paddy-fields crouching together for warmth. At a village on the coast they acquired a small native boat which they rowed down the coast until they were able to strike inland well behind our lines. I met some of these survivors in a rest camp at Ipoh. They had been badly bitten by mosquitoes on their journey. A few of them had developed great raw tropical sores from lying in the muddy water of the paddy-fields.

The only two British regiments stationed in north Malaya when the war began, the East Surreys and the Leicesters, were so badly cut up in that first engagement on the border that they lost half their effectives and had to be amalgamated into one unit which was thereafter referred to as 'the British battalion'. They were in a bad way when I met them at Ipoh. The Japanese attack at Jitra had been very much heavier than, and totally different to, anything they had expected and they had had a pretty tough time. However, they regained their spirits very quickly and fought all the way down the mainland. I had a good deal of respect for these boys of the Surreys and the Leicesters. They had none of the superficial news-values which brought publicity to the Argylls and the Australians and the Gurkhas, and they rarely made the headlines in the papers. But they stuck gamely and cheerfully to what was a heartbreakingly discouraging task. They did a good job in Malaya. I remember, a few weeks later, just before the British battalion was going in to make a counter-attack, I came across a young East Surrey lad sitting down by a stream, completely absorbed in sharpening his bayonet on a large stone. Equally absorbed by such a spectacle, I watched him in silence for several minutes. 'No-one', I remember saying to myself, 'can say that these young Londoners have not got first-rate fighting qualities.'

It is easy to give it. But to give it and be able to take it—that is the test of the good soldier. The Surreys and Leicesters both had to take it. As best they could, with what they had, they gave it.

The following English and Scottish units took part in the fighting on the mainland: the Argyll and Sutherland Highlanders, the Gordon Highlanders, the Leicesters, the East Surreys, the Loyals, the Manchesters, the Cambridgeshires, and the Norfolks. Other English regiments, which arrived during the closing stages of the campaign and fought in the defence of Singapore, were the Royal Northumberland Fusiliers, the Sherwood Foresters, the Suffolks, the Bedfordshires, and the Hertfordshires.

10

THE TACTICS OF THE JAPANESE

The Japanese not only outfought us in Malaya—they out-thought us too. In everything they showed that they had devoted considerable care and study to the special requirements of a campaign taking place in the tropical jungle of the Malayan peninsula.

Thus they wore the lightest of uniforms, a singlet, cotton shorts, rubber-soled shoes. There was no uniformity about either the colour or the form of their dress. Both dress and equipment were as light as they could be, and all our commanders agreed that their cross-country capacity was remarkable. There was no uniformity about the headgear. Various types were worn, steel helmets, cotton khaki caps, slouch hats taken from prisoners or our own dead. Often they wore Malay sarongs. Two prisoners captured near Batu Pahat were disguised as Chinese coolies. This adoption of native dress troubled our troops, since the country through which the war was being fought was fairly thickly populated and our men were never able to distinguish between friend and foe. On my first trip to the front I heard innumerable 'fifth-column' stories. The British Tommy began to think that the entire native population was fighting against him. He could never be quite certain that the young Malay lolling on the far side of the road or the Tamil coolie just disappearing into a rubber plantation was not a Japanese in disguise.

There was undoubtedly a good deal of 'fifth-column' work during the campaign. A certain number of natives were actively working with the enemy. There were well-authenticated instances of arrows, pointing to brigade or divisional headquarters, being cut in the long grass of a field, or formed of clothes hung out to dry outside a native hut, or made of large banana leaves, so that the sign could be easily picked up from the air. Certainly whenever one of our units moved to a new headquarters, the enemy usually

78

smelt it out with remarkable speed and then bombed it. But I think that the extent of the fifth-column activity was often exaggerated, especially by the British soldiery. It is always natural, when things are going badly, to pick upon scapegoats and to cry 'We are betrayed'. Undoubtedly there was a native element working actively with the enemy, but, if certain natives helped the enemy, there were many more who helped us. There are many British, Australian, and Indian soldiers who, cut off from their units, owed their safe return through the jungle to the co-operation of Malay guides, receiving food, lodging, even cigarettes from poor Chinese villagers. There were many such instances, some of which will be recounted later, especially during the later stages of the campaign. Native co-operation with the enemy in Malaya never began to assume the proportions which it assumed in Burma, for example. Most of the cases reported of Malays working with the Japanese were, in my opinion, caused by the Japanese soldiers donning sarongs. The Asiatic appearance of the enemy was also an enormous advantage to him. It enabled him to masquerade as a native of the country. The British troops would not have been able to distinguish between Chinese, Japanese, and Malays if they had been wearing their respective national dresses, let alone when they were all wearing sarongs. The Australians did the sensible thing on the east coast round Mersing. They cleared all the native inhabitants out of the area where they thought hostilities might take place. This piece of foresight was unfortunately not rewarded since the Japanese never landed at Mersing, and the Australians there, to conform with withdrawals on the west coast, had to withdraw having fired hardly a shot.

Normally the Japanese did not carry gas-masks, but an odd thing happened near Kluang later in the campaign when a detachment of Japanese were observed with gas-masks in the ready position round their necks. Shortly afterwards some Australians reported that the Japanese had used tear gas in an engagement where they were being hard-pressed. I tried unsuccessfully to obtain confirmation of this story. In China the Japanese occasionally used some sort of tear-gas bomb when they were in a tight spot. I have seen captured Japanese orders in which reference was made to a 'maru-maru' (blank-blank) shell which was presumed to be some sort of chemical projectile.

In the matter of food also the Japanese were at an advantage. Being rice-eaters, they were able to live off the country, eating the same food as the Malays and the Chinese used to eat. The British troops were dependent upon elaborate catering arrangements. There are said to be twenty-three different materials in the diet of the modern soldier. Moreover nearly all the food eaten by the white troops was tinned. I cannot believe that a sustained diet of preserved food in the tropics is good for anyone. The British soldier is in nothing more conservative than in the matter of food, but I was always surprised that so little effort was made to accustom the men to a new diet or at least to make more use of the tropical fruits and vegetables which were available in such profusion. The Japanese soldier would set off through the jungle carrying a bottle of water and a large ball of rice, with some preserved seaweed and a few pickles to make the rice palatable. Those were his rations for three or four days. The British soldier's feeding arrangements were very much more complicated.

Nearly all the Japanese infantry were armed with tommy-guns or other light automatic weapons. They were ideal for this close-range jungle fighting. Our men were armed chiefly with rifles and the percentage of automatic weapons was small. There were several bayonet engagements, a form of warfare for which the enemy seemed to have a marked distaste. Many of our officers continued to swear by the rifle right up to the end of the campaign and there are sound arguments on both sides in the rifle-versus-tommy-gun controversy. But it always seemed to me that the rifle's chief use is as an accurate long-range weapon, and in Malaya there was rarely an extended field of fire. The advanced Japanese units would carry perhaps six or eight drums of ammunition with them and further supplies would be brought up in boxes on the carriers of push-bikes.

After the tommy-gun the next most popular weapon of the enemy was a light two-inch mortar. Again, it was a weapon ideally suited to jungle warfare. It was very mobile and was easily transported and operated by two men. It was very accurate. The shell burst with a very loud report. There was also a four-inch

One of the big guns that protected the sea
approaches to Singapore

Chinese mechanics working in the foundry
at the Naval Base

A British naval vessel in the huge floating dock
at the Naval Base

The King George VI Graving-Dock,
the largest graving-dock in the Indian or Pacific Oceans

mortar which was seen mounted on armoured carriers. Except for the two-inch mortar, Japanese artillery, until the siege of Singapore, played a comparatively small part in the fighting.

Hand grenades were another weapon, extremely practicable in close fighting, of which the enemy made extensive use. Cases were reported in which Japanese climbed up trees and then tried to lob them down on to our vehicles.

Their local knowledge was excellent. They had good maps with them and their guides were mostly former Japanese residents of Malaya whose job it had been to gain a detailed knowledge of the terrain.

They were fond of arboreal tactics and snipers would often climb up trees to shoot at our outposts. One of our casualties was shot in the foot while standing in a trench three feet deep. A British officer who went after a Japanese sniper reported to be concealed in a tree told me that he felt as if he was walking up to game at home.

One of the most conspicuous features of the campaign was the great use which the Japanese made of bicycles. They may have brought some with them from Japan, but most were simply commandeered from natives in the villages, possibly being paid for in the notes which the Japanese army brought with them. (These notes were the same size, colour, and design as the British notes but said, 'The Japanese Government promises to pay the bearer on demand' the sum of ten dollars, fifty cents, or whatever the denomination was. These notes must have been printed long in advance of the outbreak of war, still further evidence of the care and thoroughness with which the Japanese planned their campaign in the Pacific. In the Philippines, in the Netherlands East Indies, in Burma, the Japanese army brought their own specially printed notes with them.) Bicycles still further increased the mobility of the Japanese and enabled their forward troops to progress at great speed.

They made full use of the numerous rivers and 'crocodile-infested' streams up-country, sometimes using collapsible rubber boats, sometimes native craft commandeered or bought from the local inhabitants, sometimes native rafts made of bamboo poles lashed together with rattan. The Chinese sampans, capable of carrying forty men and their equipment, proved ideal for entering the mangrove swamps owing to their shallow draught. The first landings at Kota Bahru were made from specially constructed iron barges, brought overland from Singora. At a later date these barges were taken overland to the Straits of Johore and used in landings on the island.

In the early stages of the campaign the Japanese used armoured carriers mounting a Bren-gun or a mortar. They would come into action on a road after Japanese infantry units had penetrated well ahead on each side of the road. The Japanese soldier, advancing stealthily and quietly through the jungle, was the spearhead of the attack, not the armoured vehicle. Later, however, on the Slim River, the Japanese brought up some medium tanks and used them in frontal attacks with telling effects. Some good photographs of these tanks can be seen in this book. The tanks had a crew of four men and mounted three cannon.

It will be seen that the highest degree of mobility was the keynote of the enemy's equipment. The British forces were nothing like so mobile. One only had to see the British soldier on his way to the front, seemingly borne down with heavy boots, tin helmet, gas-mask, heavy pack, canvas webbing, rifle and bayonet, to sense that he lacked a certain freedom of movement. He had also been trained to be very dependent on his vehicular transport and this complicated, if it did not impede, movement. One used to see British troops seemingly immobilized by their own transport.

In their tactics the Japanese practised an extreme devolution of command. Small groups of men, even single individuals, would be told to make their way as best they could to a point on the map a number of miles ahead. It would be up to them to get there. They would set off through the jungle, quietly picking their way, sometimes lying concealed for hours. Arrived at the given point behind our lines they would re-form. Contact with their forces in the rear would be maintained by portable wireless apparatus. If they came up against one of our outposts, they would attack it from the front, but, if the opposition were severe, would make no attempt to press home the frontal attack. Instead, they would creep round and attack it either from the flank or from the rear. Similarly, if our troops advanced, the enemy would simply melt into the jungle on each side and again attack from the flank. Such were the tactics employed by the Japanese not only against sections but against whole brigades and divisions. The landings on the west coast which later caused us so much trouble, when sometimes one or two thousand men would slip ashore under cover of darkness, were simply attempts to outflank our positions on a much larger scale.

These tactics were made possible by several things—by the Japanese superiority in numbers; by the fact that the terrain in Malaya favoured the attacker at every turn and hindered the defender; by the remarkable cross-country capacity of the Japanese infantryman who was the spearhead of the attack; by the enemy's superior local knowledge.

The following three instances may perhaps give some idea of the 'confused' fighting which was caused by these 'infiltrating tactics' as they came to be called. At one point a bridge was just about to be demolished when three Japanese motor-cyclists came dashing over and actually succeeded in driving straight up to divisional headquarters. One was promptly shot by the then divisional commander, Major-General Murray Lyon, who had drawn his revolver. Another was shot by a member of the staff. The third escaped. At another place, long inside our lines, a Japanese suddenly popped up from a paddy-field, again only a few hundred yards away from a brigade headquarters. Our men, who had been in the vicinity for some time, calculated that he must have been lying in the muddy water for at least six hours. At a third place two British dispatch-riders were riding down a road in the forward zone when they were ambushed by Japanese who had filtered through. One was shot dead. The other had his petrol tank punctured and escaped. The body of the dead dispatch-rider was later retrieved by two Gurkhas. Transport ambushed on the road, outposts surprised in the jungle, battalion headquarters suddenly attacked in the dead of night—these things happened over and over again.

There are no sure means of countering such tactics. The advanced outposts must have strict orders never to give way but to hold to their positions at all costs, and there must be sufficient bodies of men operating behind the lines to mop up the parties of infiltrating troops. Unfortunately there were never enough

British troops at any one phase of the campaign on the mainland for this to be done. If there had been two or three times the number of British troops available on the west coast, it might have been possible to check the Japanese advance. But this again is slightly defensive thinking. Actually I doubt if there is any means of countering infiltrating tactics by the enemy except by infiltrating in the opposite direction against him, and this at least requires a certain equality of numbers, mobility, and equipment.

The whole question of numbers is tremendously important. Our forces in Malaya were really divided up into four groups. The 9th Indian Division was on the east coast, chiefly at Kota Bahru and Kuantan. The 11th Division was fighting the campaign down the west coast. The 8th Australian Division (only two brigades) was in Johore guarding the land approaches to Singapore. A few battalions were kept in reserve at Singapore. (One whole division arrived in Singapore during January.)

The Japanese are believed to have begun their attack on Malaya with four divisions, using two in the Kota Bahru area and two in Kedah. A fifth was known to be kept in reserve at Singora. It may have been the division of Imperial Guards which was later thrown into battle against the Australians in the Muar sector. (A Japanese division has twenty thousand men, incidentally, compared with fifteen thousand in a British division.) I know that some highly qualified observers maintain that the Japanese never used more than three divisions on the mainland and that all this talk of the enemy's superiority in numbers was really a lame excuse for ineffective tactics. Certainly the capture of Singapore was effected by a numerically inferior enemy. (At Singapore there were other factors of equipment, air strength, and morale.) We shall only know the true numbers involved on the other side when Japanese writers after the war give their recollections with the same accuracy and dispassion that I am trying to observe in this narrative.

Personally I believe that the figures quoted above are substantially correct, namely, that the enemy used four divisions in the attack on Malaya and added a fifth when he came to Johore. But, whether they are correct or not, it is indisputable that on the mainland the enemy nearly always contrived to enjoy a *local numerical superiority*. Even when this did not mean that our forces were opposed by numerically superior forces, it meant that the Japanese forces had had some rest and were fresh, whereas most of our forces fought for weeks without any let-up at all.

We failed, as I have already shown, to take the initiative against the enemy during the first few days of the war. There were some observers, including experienced military strategists, who held that, having failed to advance north or hold the enemy on the Thai border, we should have withdrawn all our forces to the Johore line (formed roughly by the road running across the peninsula from Mersing, through Kluang, to Batu Pahat) and engaged the enemy in force there, leaving just a small force to delay the enemy's advance down the peninsula. This school of thought also held that Singapore could not be held if the Johore line went, and that, once it went, it was the right thing, not only *not* to reinforce Singapore, but also to evacuate as many troops and as much equipment as possible to Java.

As it was, we compromised. Two divisions fought a delaying action down the mainland which prevented the Japanese from coming up against the Johore line until January 15th. The purpose of this action was presumably to enable reinforcements to be poured into Singapore. Unfortunately the losses incurred during this delaying action were unduly heavy, some of our best units like the Argyll and Sutherland Highlanders and the Gurkhas losing 75 per cent of their men. The two divisions were completely exhausted by the time they reached Johore and moreover had acquired the psychology of withdrawal, if not of defeat. The positions on the Johore line were so weakened that the six Australian battalions (two of which were out of the show completely on the east coast) went into action with comparatively little support. Again in Johore we were faced with a local Japanese numerical superiority.

Professional and amateur strategists will probably wrangle about this problem for years to come. Should we have advanced into Thailand? Failing to advance into Thailand, should we have fallen back on Johore and massed our strength there for a major engagement? Failing to hold the Japanese in Johore, should we have evacuated Singapore and tried to hold Java?

The Tactics of the Japanese

Many more facts will be required before proper answers can be given. My own feelings are that we should have advanced into Thailand and that, failing to do so, we should have then fallen back on Johore. I do not think that the ultimate outcome of the campaign would have been any different. Singapore would have still fallen to the enemy. The situation in Malaya had so many ingredients of calamity from the British point of view that only calamity could have resulted. But I think that, with all our resources massed in Johore, we should have put up a better show. Singapore would not have passed from our control in quite such a humiliating manner.

The Tactics of the Japanese

11

THE WAR IN THE AIR

During the first trip to the Malayan front that I made as a war correspondent there was one cry which went up from every soldier I met—'Give us air support.'

'We're doing our best,' they would say, 'but we can't do much without air support.' In the opinion of the British ground troops lack of air support was the prime reason for the débâcle.

In nothing had we underestimated the Japanese more than in the air. We did not realize that their bombing tactics could be as formidable as they proved, despite the fact that our observers had been able to study these tactics during the four and a half years of unopposed target practice that the Japanese air force had in China. We did not know what sort of fighter planes they had but we did not believe that what they had could be much good. A few weeks before the war started I remember Sir Robert Brooke-Popham saying at a press conference that, although our fighter planes in Malaya were admittedly not the fastest in the world, we believed them to be adequate to deal with anything that the Japanese could produce. The little Japanese Navy 0 turned out to be a complete surprise.

Three factors were responsible for this lamentable underestimation of the enemy's air strength. First, and probably most important, the Japanese, during the previous two years, had learned a lot from the Germans. How much they had learned we could only tell after the war started. It was known that there had been many Nazi technical experts in Japan showing the Japanese the latest German methods of plane production and design. German influence was clearly apparent in the design and tactics of some of the planes which the Japanese used over Malaya, although there were also many features which were purely Japanese. Secondly, the elaborate, often comically elaborate, steps which the Japanese used to take to protect their naval, military, and aerial secrets undoubtedly contributed to the fact that our Intelligence was nothing like so exact or comprehensive as was their Intelligence in regard to the British and American dispositions. Lastly, it had become the habit to disparage Japanese capabilities in the air. Absurd myths came into being. The Japanese could not possibly be good flyers because they had bad eyesight, because they suffered from vertigo caused by riding on their mother's backs when babies. Even experts who knew Japan and the Japanese often tended to underestimate the Japanese because, perhaps unconsciously, they had the feeling that the East could never achieve equal mastery with the West of machines that had been invented, designed, and developed in the West. Living in Tokyo there were so many superficial characteristics of the Japanese that seemed to bear out that contention. The only commercial car which the Japanese had produced in any quantity, a pseudo-Austin 7 called a Datsun, was a dreadful little tin can, always going out of order. The ordinary Tokyo taxi-driver at the wheel of a Ford or Dodge maltreated his vehicle almost as sadistically as his counterpart in China. If the people could not manufacture a decent commercial car, if they could not even handle properly the American cars which they imported in such numbers, it seemed improbable that they would be able to manufacture and handle aeroplanes (with their infinitely more intricate mechanism) which could equal those which were being manufactured in the West.

The Japanese used the following chief types of plane during the campaign in Malaya:

1. *The Navy* 96. A Mitsubishi-built twin-engined bomber carrying a crew of five which was used in the large-scale formation raids.

2. *The Army* 97. Another Mitsubishi-built twin-engined bomber, with a longer nose than the Navy 96, which was also used, although to a lesser extent, in the big raids.

3. *The Junkers* 88. A fast-flying twin-engined plane with retractable undercarriage and a crew of three. It was an exact replica, made in Japan, of the German plane.

4. *The Junkers Ju* 87B. This was the dive-bomber which used to operate chiefly over the fighting zones. Of the same design as its

German prototype, it had certain slight modifications in armament.

5. *The Navy* 97. A torpedo-carrying plane capable of operating from an aircraft-carrier. Planes of this type, based on Saigon, sank the *Prince of Wales* and the *Repulse*.

6. *The Navy* 0. This little single-engined fighter was the surprise of the aerial side of the war. It had been used against the Chinese in the spring of 1941 and details of it had been sent home by American correspondents in Chungking, and were probably available to other Air Attachés. However, its performance no doubt surprised the experts. It was of the lightest construction: the Japanese took the best aeroplane engine available, incorporating details from many sources, appended a light silk-over-aluminium frame, and achieved the most manœuvrable plane in the world. The pilot has no armour or protection; there are machine-guns (and a cannon in later models) but one hit is enough to bring the Navy 0 down. It is quite unlike the fast fighters of Britain, America, and Germany: its merits are featherweight construction, manœuvrability, and its power to climb almost vertically if necessary.

The Japanese bombing was of two kinds.

The raids on airfields and docks and the Naval Base in Singapore were carried out at an altitude of 17,000 to 25,000 feet by big formations of twenty-one, twenty-four, or twenty-seven planes, flying in one large V or three smaller Vs. Sometimes one of these formations would be followed by one or more similar formations. Raids on the airfields up-country were carried out by smaller groups of nine, twelve, or fifteen planes. The formations were absolutely flawless. To us who had been in Japan it seemed strange that a people who find it congenitally difficult to march in step should yet have learned to keep in step so perfectly in the air. Arrived over the target the commander of the formation (flying, however, not in the leading plane), would give the order by wireless to release the bombs, which would all be dropped simultaneously. It was a safe and sure method of bombing for, when some two hundred bombs are dropped at regular intervals over an area of one square mile, the chances are that a few of them will do some damage. After the first Japanese formation raid on the airfield of Sembawang on Singapore Island no less than 125 craters were counted on and near the airfield. If a bomber was hit by anti-aircraft fire from the ground and was obliged to break formation, the plane behind would move up and take its place. The formations would usually be escorted by fighters flying so high above that they were not visible with the naked eye to people on the ground. If British fighters flew up to break the formation, the Japanese fighters would swoop down from above. If the British fighters succeeded nevertheless in approaching the bombers, the Japanese machine-gunners would all fire together and put up quite a formidable barrage. If the bombers were attacked from the side, the planes on one side would dip while those on the other side would rise so that they could fire their barrage to the side instead of upwards. It was pattern-bombing raids of this sort which were made upon the docks at Singapore, upon the Naval Base, upon the island's five airfields, upon the *Prince of Wales* and the *Repulse*, upon shipping in Singapore harbour, upon the airfields up-country, and occasionally upon other objectives. I remember a pattern bombing of Johore Bahru when corps headquarters was located there, another of the Australian headquarters off Bukit Timah road after the siege of the island had begun, a few pattern bombings of the civilian areas of Singapore city.

The bombing in the forward areas, which caused our men to plead so incessantly for air support, was carried out chiefly by dive-bombers, operating either singly or in groups of three or five. They did not go into that steep vertical dive of the German Stuka. Their dive was a short and shallow one, sufficient, however, to enable the bomb-aimer to get a line on his target. The chief objectives of these dive-bombers were transport on the roads, artillery positions, any headquarters which they had located, concentrations of troops, the railway, ships off the coast, and so forth. After releasing the bombs these planes would cruise up and down with the rear gunner blazing away at anything he could see. This was a type of aerial attack to which all the men up at the front were subjected. Usually one just lay flat on the ground, under cover if there was any available, and hoped for the best.

The Japanese bombers dropped various types of bombs. In the pattern bombing carried out by the big formations the bombs were usually mixed. Very few heavy bombs were dropped. The biggest craters I saw in Malaya were only some twenty-five feet across and perhaps ten feet deep. Most of the bombs were light fragmentation bombs. They had no penetrating power. If they fell on an asphalt road, they would sometimes not even penetrate the asphalt, although the surface would be marked with a radial pattern showing where the splinters had shot out in all directions. But if they had no penetrating power, they compensated for it by a tremendous lateral range. Fragments would fly for 200 yards, would be burning hot when picked up, with edges razor sharp. It actually happened on one occasion that a plane was set on fire and burnt out by a fragment from a bomb which fell 450 yards away. They were fairly effective missiles. They could do great damage on an airfield if there were planes scattered around on the ground, and they were sufficiently explosive to cause considerable havoc amongst the jerry-built brick and timber dwellings of the native quarters of Singapore. It was reported that a long rod was affixed to the nose of the bomb, with the result that the bomb exploded in the air when the end of the rod touched the ground. A variation of the fragmentation bomb was the anti-personnel bomb or 'daisy-cutter' which was dropped on our men at the front. Neither type had any penetrating power, but whereas the fragments of the first type would explode upwards and outwards, the fragments of the 'daisy-cutter' would spread parallel to the ground. Various types of incendiary bomb were used but never in very large quantities.

During the first two weeks of the war the Japanese bombers and fighters operated from Saigon. The escorting fighters carried extra fuel tanks to give them increased range. The tanks would be dropped when the petrol in them had been consumed. They were five feet long, shaped like torpedoes, and made of aluminium. After two weeks the Japanese planes began to use the field at Alor Star and then the airfields further south as the Japanese forces advanced down the peninsula. When based on Saigon the bombers could make only one raid on Singapore each day; when based on Kuala Lumpur they could make two or three.

The Japanese fighter planes were flown with skill and daring. The quality of the Japanese Navy 0 was as much a surprise as was the poor quality of the American-built Brewster Buffalo, when the two were finally pitted against each other. The Buffaloes, which were the only fighter planes in Singapore for the first month of the war, turned out to be far slower than the Navy 0's, less manœuvrable, less efficiently armed. They were a bitter disappointment. Large numbers were out of commission when the hostilities began. Those that went into action were shot up by the Japanese and many were destroyed on the ground during Japanese bombing attacks on the airfields in north Malaya. Those few Buffaloes that survived the first week of war were withdrawn to Singapore. Thus there were no British fighters during those early stages to break up the big enemy formations, to impede the dive-bombers in the forward zones who had the air literally to themselves, and to provide fighter escort for our bombers. It was a pathetic situation. The only thing the Air Force did achieve during those early weeks was to provide a certain amount of aerial reconnaissance. No enemy convoys came anywhere near Malaya unreported and some excellent photographs were taken of enemy airfields. The Hurricanes, which first took the air about the middle of January, arrived too late and in insufficient quantities. Of the fifty odd which arrived in crates, I doubt if half ever took to the air, the rest being destroyed on the ground, some of them still in their crates. I never saw more than seven Hurricanes in the air at one time over Malaya. Plane for plane they were a match for the Navy 0. The British plane had the edge in speed and could dive with greater speed because it was heavier. The Japanese plane had the edge in manœuvrability and the advantage when it came to a dog-fight. Our planes therefore (like the American P-40s later in Java and northern Australia) tried to avoid dog-fights and instead would mount to a height and then make one long swoop upon the enemy, plunge through the formation with all guns firing, dive down, climb up again, and try to repeat the performance. The trouble about the Hurricanes was that they were always outnumbered. Quality was equal at last but numbers were not. And, as happened to the Buffaloes, many more were destroyed on the ground than were ever destroyed in combat in the air. Some observers held that three squadrons of Hurricanes might successfully have challenged the enemy's control of the air. If we had had 250 fighter planes in Malaya, there never would have been any campaign at all, for the enemy would never have been able to set foot on Kota Bahru. Fighters and Hudsons together wrought tremendous havoc during the early hours of the Japanese landing there.

The Japanese aerial personnel who were taken prisoner suggested that they are the *élite* in the enemy's armed forces, as is the case with Germany and also, to a large extent, with ourselves. It is not true that the Japanese fly without parachutes. Nor is it true that in the big bombing formations only the commander's plane is equipped with all the proper navigational instruments. But it is true that one Japanese fighter pilot, who crashed in Johore, climbed out of his plane, and, after holding back a group of curious Malays, pulled a pistol out of its holster, put it to his head, and shot himself. The flyers are perhaps the most fanatical of any section of the Japanese forces.

In fairness to the enemy it must be admitted that the Japanese in Malaya, whatever they may have done in China, Burma, and other theatres of war, did confine themselves by and large to military objectives. There were certain lapses. There were the raids on Penang already described, which, in my opinion, were acts of deliberate terrorism intended to spread panic and alarm throughout the native peoples of the Malayan peninsula. There were five or six bad raids on the native quarters of Singapore for which there can be no excuse. Cities and towns on the mainland, fifty or sixty miles behind the front, were usually subjected to one small-scale raid just to clear out the civilian population. But, broadly speaking, the Japanese confined their bombing to legitimate military objectives, and the number of civilian casualties was comparatively small when one considers the constant aerial activity.

Airfields were the chief objective, then docks. The raids on the airfields certainly achieved their aim. They put them out of action and destroyed large numbers of our machines on the ground. At that time we had not learned how to disperse our bombers into runways in the jungle. Every airfield on Singapore had several charred remnants of planes. Later in Java I remember visiting the Bandoeng airfield just after a raid by a formation of fourteen Japanese planes and finding four Flying Fortresses put out of action by flying splinters from fragmentation bombs. For every

British plane destroyed in the air over Malaya there must have been at least four destroyed on the ground.

In some respects the Japanese aerial command displayed a remarkable lack of imagination and initiative. It was a perpetual mystery to our military commanders why the Japanese did not bomb our communications more. I cannot remember a single bridge behind our lines being put out of action by enemy bombing. There were never any blockages on the roads caused by bombing. The British sappers spent all their time on demolishing, never on repairing, bridges. We depended to an enormous extent on motorized transport. One small bridge temporarily destroyed would have caused transport to pile up for miles on either side, such traffic jams providing excellent targets. A couple of bombs on the Johore causeway any time during the last three weeks that we were fighting on the mainland could have caused appalling chaos. Transport was sometimes machine-gunned and roads bombed in the forward areas. But there was never any attempt to disrupt our communications in the rear. The popular explanation was that the Japanese felt so certain of their triumphant advance that they did not want to damage unduly roads which they would want to use afterwards themselves. But this struck me as a stupid argument since we blew up all bridges anyway as we withdrew. I put it down to those curious blind spots which are such a conspicuous feature of the Japanese national character.

In brief it may be said that early in the campaign the Japanese established an almost complete ascendancy in the air. It was challenged, but only briefly, when the Hurricanes first went into action. Of all the factors responsible for the débâcle it was perhaps the most decisive. It had various effects, of which the least important, so it seemed to me, was the material damage done to military and naval installations. (The damage done to aerial installations was, of course, great.) This ascendancy in the air enabled the Japanese to carry out aerial reconnaissance at their leisure and thereby further augment their Intelligence. It enabled them to use aeroplanes as forward observation posts for artillery on the ground. Most important of all, it had a great moral effect upon the British troops, especially upon the Indians. The latter had always been told in their training that, when they eventually went into action against a real enemy, they would have air support. Good troops will take an enormous amount of punishment, and they will continue to take it, if they know that the enemy is receiving even just a particle of what they are receiving. But to fight day after day, week after week, to be machine-gunned and bombed continuously from the air, to watch the enemy planes circling around with complete impunity, never to see a British plane at all, let alone a British plane tackling the enemy—it is easy to see how the balance of power in the air, when taken in conjunction with other adverse factors, eventually had a most dispiriting effect upon the morale of the British troops. There was a true story of a British ack-ack gunner who saw a plane in the sky and began to loose off at it, when it was pointed out to him that he was firing, not at a Japanese but at a British plane. 'I don't believe it,' he said. 'It can't be true,' and continued to fire his gun.

The absurd thing was that the Japanese achieved this almost unchallenged control of the air with an aerial strength that is by no means great. I reckoned that, during the whole Malayan campaign, including aircraft of every type, the Japanese used a total of only five hundred planes. This figure probably errs on the generous side. It was not the Japanese who were strong. It was ourselves who were weak, pathetically weak. I do not believe that the Japanese are strong in the air when judged by German, Russian, American, or present British standards. But they were able to concentrate their main aerial strength, first of all in Malaya, then in the Indies, then in Burma. They had noticed the way in which Hitler used to concentrate on one theatre of war at a time. It has been, and still is, the great weakness of the Allied war effort that our striking power has been so dispersed. Our aerial strength was divided between the home front, the Middle East, Russia, and Malaya. However appalled we may be by the poverty of the British aerial resources in Malaya at the start of the Pacific war, it is important to remember that Malaya came fourth on the priority list. Accepting the fact of our complete unpreparedness when war broke out in Europe, an unpreparedness which Mr. Churchill inherited on becoming Prime Minister, it is very difficult to argue that Malaya during 1940 and 1941 should have taken precedence over either Britain, the Middle East, or Russia, in the allotment of the products of the British and American aircraft factories.

And yet, incredibly grim as was the situation in the air over Malaya, I deduced from it the chief auguries of eventual Allied success. If control of the air could make as much difference as it did in Malaya, what might the situation not be like when *we* wrest that control from the enemy? Allied success depends, in my opinion, largely on American aircraft production. Whatever the present relative aerial strength of Japan and the United States may be, there can be no question whose is the greater potential strength. When a country that has turned out automobiles by the million begins to turn out aircraft by the hundred thousand, will it not be our turn to hunt the Japanese out of the skies, to bomb *their* airfields and destroy *their* aircraft on the ground?

Not only did the Japanese drop bombs on Malaya; they also dropped leaflets by the thousand, in every language spoken in the peninsula, English, Malay, Chinese, Hindustani, Urdu, Gurmukhi. The leaflets were usually remarkable as much for the fatuity of their contents as for the incorrectness of the idiom in which they were couched. From a Japanese aircraft, flying so high that it was invisible to the naked eye, they would flutter down out of the sky on Singapore or on the towns up-country. I remember one in English, purporting to be a newspaper extra and carrying a spurious Lisbon date-line, which declared that the United States had opened separate peace negotiations with Japan. Another, addressed to the officers and men of the British Army, asked, 'Why do you submit to the intolerable torture of malarial mosquitoes merely to pamper the British aristocrat? Do not dedicate your lives merely to fatten the British high-hat.' One addressed to the Indian troops would show a British officer sheltering in the rear while the Indians fought the enemy. One in Malay would contain a crude drawing of a fat white man with a whisky-glass in his hand treading a Malay under foot, or a map of the Malayan peninsula with the Rising Sun flags all round it and the Union Jack flying only in the middle of the peninsula. One addressed to the Australians showed a blonde floozy tossing restlessly on her bed and crying out, 'Oh, Johnny, come back to me. I am so lonely without you.' One dropped on Singapore on Christmas Day had a

A specimen of the money the Japanese
brought with them to Malaya

Sacks of rice being distributed to the workers
on a rubber estate

Tamils going into the jungle as hostilities near their homes
—a common sight up-country

After an air-raid on the civil airport at Kalang
smoke drifts over the city

drawing of what looked like several cavemen brandishing torches, with the legend underneath in Chinese and Malay—'Burn all the white devils in the sacred white flame of victory.' Bedrock in crudity was reached with a leaflet containing a reprint of a letter taken from the body of a dead Australian, written by his wife in Australia and giving him all the news about home and children. Pamphlets of this nature simply made the few white men who saw them feel that they were pitted against a brutal and barbaric foe. A pamphlet of another type, however, had a certain effect on the Asiatic population. One which fell on Singapore simply advised the native population to evacuate the city on a certain date. Fearing a terrific blitz on the date mentioned a certain number of natives did evacuate, causing, if they were labourers or men engaged on essential services, still further complications in the problem of native labour. The day in question passed quite uneventfully nor was the scale of Japanese air attacks noticeably intensified during the days following. Occasionally the natives received advance information whether there was going to be a raid that day or not, and the British staff at aerodromes would always prepare for a raid if they noticed any unusual movement on the part of the native inhabitants.

12

MEMORIES OF NORTH MALAYA

Let me put down, before they fade for ever, a few of my memories of those trips to the front in Malaya. Life in the zones behind the lines was completely crazy, only one did not think of it as being crazy.

We arrived at Ipoh one day and went to the Majestic Hotel for lunch. There had been two raids on the airfield that morning and some bombs had fallen on the town, with the result that the entire staff of the hotel had vanished. Self-appointed manager was a drunken middle-aged Scotsman, possibly a planter from up-country, evacuating south in a car filled with his worldly possessions. With him was his native mistress, a woman called Rose, who told us that her father had been born and brought up in Thailand. 'I suppose,' she explained, in her not very good English, 'I'm what most people would call a bastard.' She was completely devoted to 'her man' who was wandering round the hotel with a loaded shotgun.

We helped ourselves to drinks from the bar and then dug up some food from the kitchen. The radio had been left on and was blaring out dance music through the empty hotel rooms. At intervals bombs could be heard exploding. And the drunken Scotsman tottered unsteadily round with his shotgun under his arm, looking out from his bloodshot little pig eyes, and Rose reminisced about her early life in Thailand and told us how cleverly she could outwit Chinese shopkeepers when they tried to gyp her.

*   *   *

The officer commanding the British forces in north Malaya was Lieutenant-General Sir Lewis Heath, who had come out with the 3rd Indian Corps. 'Piggy' Heath, as he was known to his men, was the victor of Keren and had played a distinguished part in the war in Africa. He was completely imperturbable under fire and, although corps headquarters was in Kuala Lumpur, he used to spend much of his time in the forward zones. Although he could not be described as an inspirational leader, he was known to the men under his command and trusted by them.

Heath was always very decent to the Press, as indeed were nearly all the senior commanders actually in the field. He had a keen mind and would always give us a most·enlightening and complete picture of the military situation. I remember one very telling phrase he once used: 'The Japanese are formidable opponents because they combine the cunning and resourcefulness of the tribesmen of the north-west frontier of India with the discipline and direction of the modern army.'

Heath was a big man with a withered left arm, the result of a wound in the last war. (His chief-of-staff had also, curiously enough, lost the use of his left arm.) He was an able commander, but he had been assigned a heart-breaking task. Already, two weeks after the start of the war, the strain was evident in his worn, weary, parchment-coloured face.

*   *   *

A man whom the correspondents loved to interview was Colonel Ian Stewart, officer commanding the Argyll and Sutherland Highlanders, later placed in command of a brigade. He was succeeded in the command of his battalion by Lieutenant-Colonel Robertson, who had been Military Aide-de-camp to Mr. Duff Cooper. (Robertson, a man of great ability and strong views, was reported missing after the tank engagement on the Slim River and was almost certainly killed there.)

Ian Stewart had the reputation of being a strict disciplinarian. Some months before the war started he made his men march down to Singapore from Mersing, a distance of some hundred miles, which they covered, I believe, in six days. Officers had to march too, nor were the drivers of the battalion's Bren-gun carriers and motorized transport allowed to escape. On reaching Singapore all drivers had to march an equivalent distance round the island. Certainly Stewart brought his men up to a tremendous pitch of fitness and efficiency. He was not only a most able soldier but a man of the greatest personal charm.

Memories of North Malaya

Various short accounts have been written of the record of the Argylls during the campaign in Malaya. It is to be hoped that a full and authoritative account will eventually be written. It will be an important document and will tell a stirring tale. Originally part of the Singapore garrison, the Argylls, were moved up to the front quite early in the campaign when things began to go badly for us. They first went into action on the Grik road in Perak, and then fought in the engagements on the west coast in Perak and Selangor. Terribly badly cut up on the Slim River, they fell back with the rest of the British forces to Johore, and helped to cover the withdrawal on to the island. Two hundred were then left out of some 850 men. They were the last troops to leave the mainland and marched across the Johore causeway by night with their pipes playing. When dispositions were allotted on the island, the Argylls formed part of Command reserves. The morning after the Japanese landed they were pushed up into that very sector in the north-west of the island where the Australians were trying unsuccessfully to hold the Japanese assault. Three officers finally evaded capture and made their way to Sumatra: Stewart himself, Angus Rose, who had been organizing and taking part in the commando operations behind the enemy's lines, and a subaltern called, if I remember rightly, Taylor. He had a slight shrapnel wound in his head when I met him in Batavia. A few of the men also made their escape. The true figures of the personnel who survived the campaign and the full story of their gallant achievement will only be known after the war.

Stewart was already a brigadier when I first met him one morning at the front. He was tall, lean, and active, with piercing blue eyes, a glengarry with the silver regimental badge jauntily perched on the side of his head. Brigade headquarters was in a pleasant European house, the residence of some government official who had moved south, and the chief item of news that morning was the story of a remarkable hand-to-hand engagement that had taken place in a railway station just up the line.

A young captain in the Argylls, who was formerly a reserve rugby forward for Scotland, together with his sergeant-major and his orderly, drove to an advanced outpost at a station south of Ipoh to inspect and carry some rations to a section on duty there. Suddenly they saw a party of about fifteen Japanese sneaking into the far end of the station guided by a Tamil coolie. A larger party with bicycles could be seen in the distance, coming up the line. The Argylls decided to attack. The captain ordered the section to cover the flank while he and his two companions launched a frontal assault. The C.S.M. and the orderly opened with tommy-guns. A bloody scrap then began actually in the buildings of the station. Coming across some Japanese in one of the rooms, the captain, his Highland blood thoroughly aroused, threw away his rifle and attacked the Japanese with his hands. The C.S.M. joined in the fray. He had run out of ammunition but seized his tommy-gun by the barrel and laid about him with its butt. The Japanese kicked and bit and fought furiously. One who was proving particularly troublesome was dealt with by the captain who bashed him on the head with his tin helmet and knocked him unconscious. Having cleared up the station, the Scots then made a getaway in their lorry, actually bringing with them the Japanese who had been knocked unconscious. Altogether these three men, aided by covering fire from the section, killed at least twelve of the enemy without suffering so much as a scratch themselves.

The captain was out when we arrived at battalion headquarters, but we met the C.S.M. He was the mildest of men and it was difficult to picture him in the savage role which he had played at the station. The palms of his hands were blistered from holding the burning-hot barrel of his tommy-gun.

What a delightful group of people they were, those young officers of the Argylls! Tired and worn after several days of pretty continuous action, but still amazingly cheerful. They were drawn from the oldest families in Scotland. There was a 'spirit of the regiment' which you could sense at once. When I hear people inveighing against the degeneracy of my contemporaries, especially those contemporaries who come from the old familes of England and have been to the old schools, I like to think (although I know there is something in what the critics say) of those young officers of the Argylls in their battalion headquarters in the middle of the Malayan jungle. They were fighting just as doggedly as their fathers or grandfathers ever fought in the wars before them. I doubt if a single officer whom I met there that day survived the war in Malaya. And the men, too. Dour, stocky little men, speaking a tongue so remote from ordinary English that an Englishman had to listen hard to understand everything they said. Taken often from the slums of the big Scottish cities, where they had early learned that life is a fight from start to finish, they had been moulded by the discipline and tradition of the regiment into a force that any commander would be proud to have under him. The relationship between officer and man was the old traditional relationship (as different as anything could be from the new democratic relationship that exists amongst the Australians, for example) at its very best and its most efficient.

While we were at battalion headquarters an old Chinese was brought in. He was gibbering with fear. Two privates said that some three hundred yards away just outside this man's hut they had come across a large arrow, made of banana leaves laid out on the grass, pointing in the direction of the headquarters. It was on an open stretch of grass and the arrow would have been clearly visible to an aeroplane flying overhead. The old man was interrogated by an Intelligence officer who knew Chinese. His answers were not satisfactory. He was taken out. A minute later a single shot rang out. It was 'rough justice', but men who are engaged upon this business of killing and avoiding being killed have not time for anything else.

*　　　　*　　　　*

Sikh soldiers at the front, going up to the front line or coming back out of action to take up positions further in the rear, tired, worn, their uniforms torn and stained. Magnificent bearded men, of a patriarchal dignity, sitting beneath the rubber trees, with their rifles over their knees. Slim young men whose faces, never touched by razor, were just beginning to sprout a thin curling beard.

I often wondered what was going on in the minds of these men. They could not be filled by any particular hatred of the Japanese. Their horizons were too limited to see that Malaya was the eastern defence outpost of their native land. Nor could they be inspired by any particular devotion to their British rulers. They were not politically minded one way or the other. No. They fought because

Sikhs had always fought. Their fathers had been in the regiment, their grandfathers before them. Behind them was a warrior tradition reaching back into antiquity. Sikhs fought because fighting was in their blood and being. Besides, there was the reputation of the regiment, the family, and the individual to be maintained; there were brothers and cousins and comrades in the Army, who could not be let down.

It was a type of fighting that was new and distasteful to them. 'These Indians are fighting blind,' Major-General Barstow, officer commanding the 9th Division, told me. 'They feel they have a hood over the eyes.' It was utterly different from the fighting in Africa, where the spaces were wide and open and you could see your enemy. In this jungle fighting the first you knew of your enemy was when he fired at you from out of a thick clump of bushes fifty yards away. You didn't know where he was. He might be to the side of you, behind you, up a tree actually above you.

The impression which the Indian troops chiefly gave was one of bewilderment. And yet, such were their innate martial qualities, such the moulding power of the long years of army discipline, that they continued to fight as they had been taught to fight and never flinched, even when dispirited and physically exhausted, from going up to face the enemy again.

*　　　　*　　　　*

I remember a story of the Indian doctors at the hospital at Ipoh. Constant Japanese aerial activity eventually made the continuation of normal hospital work impossible. Many patients, mostly air-raid casualties, were taken to a hospital further south by the British medical officers. Four of the Indian doctors, however, decided to take seventy of the most urgent and serious cases to Tanjong Rambutan, fifteen miles north-east of Ipoh, where was located the largest lunatic asylum in Malaya. The hospital there had over 3,000 beds and an attached farm made it largely self-supporting in food. There they would await the coming of the Japanese forces.

At a later date, the hospital at Kuala Lumpur was left in charge of the Indian staff while the British personnel moved south. The old British doctor at the leper colony north of Kuala Lumpur decided, however, to stay with his charges. So did the British lay superintendent.

British personnel in the medical services, as well as in all the other services, had orders to proceed south when they judged the time had come to do so. I still remember the feeling of intense shame which I experienced when talking to the senior Indian medical officer at Kuala Lumpur. He was staying, the British doctors were going. He would have to meet the Japanese soldiers when they first drove up to the hospital and demanded, in all probability, to search the hospital. He would have to keep the native staff together as best as he could. He would have to look after the seventeen recently born babies. When we said good-bye, we shook hands and wished each other luck—but I could hardly bear to look him in the eyes.

The British doctors from up-country would usually say: 'But we could not carry on our work. All our native staff ran away. We were having to do everything ourselves, prepare the food, even bury the bodies.' At the same time I cannot help feeling that a doctor's duty to his patients is so great that he ought to stay with them no matter what orders he receives, even if it means that he is not allowed to carry on his work but is put in a concentration camp.

Fear was behind a good number of the untimely withdrawals on the part of British officials and residents up-country. One or two Japanese atrocity stories had got around. A British planter in Kelantan was reported to have been found tied to a tree, done to death in the most horrible fashion. The Japanese themselves broadcast far and wide that they were fighting only against the white people, not against the natives. It was easy to imagine how British residents in Malaya who had never been to Japan or China, who had only known Japanese photographers and Chinese shop-keepers, now pictured the Japanese as being incarnations of cruelty and brutality. And of course in many cases these people's jobs had simply dried up on them and there was no particular reason why they should stay. At the same time I felt strongly that more of the doctors should have stayed and that more of the officials and planters should not have left quite as early as they did.

Memories of North Malaya

The plea 'I want to get somewhere where I can be of some use' became rather monotonous after a time. The Dutch in the Indies stayed with their people longer, although there is admittedly in several of the Dutch islands a hinterland to which these people could retire and live, whereas there was no such hinterland in Malaya.

* * *

One of the things that bothered me a great deal when I first became a correspondent was the terrible inaccuracy that nine men out of ten display when they recount what they have seen or what they have done. But when we were at the front we usually had to send off our stories the same night and we did not have time to do a lot of checking and cross-checking.

A correspondent obviously must be motivated by the highest regard for truth and accuracy. He must strive continuously for these things. He must train himself to be accurate in his thinking, accurate in his reporting. He must be dispassionate, objective. But he must also accept the limitations of his profession. All newspapermen, including war correspondents, have to work against time, often at the greatest pressure. There is not time for half that checking and cross-checking that one would like to be able to do. Life is too short, inaccuracies are bound to occur in one's dispatches. The important thing is that the *striving* for accuracy should be there and that one's mind should be free of those things that make for inaccuracy.

* * *

Quite early in the campaign stories began to circulate that the Japanese had white officers with them. I met a jemadar of a Sikh regiment, a great big bearded fellow, who had come in one day with a tommy-gun and a long Japanese sword which he claimed to have captured in curious circumstances. He said that he had been out with the havildar-major in the front line some fourteen miles north of Ipoh when they were fired on from behind a tree by a tall blond man in khaki uniform. The white man killed the havildar but was in turn killed by the jemadar. The latter tried to bring back the body but the approach of enemy troops obliged him to beat a hasty retreat, and he brought only the gun and the sword which the man was carrying. The Sikh was a large man but he said the dead white man was very much larger and so heavy it was difficult to lift him.

Another Sikh jemadar who was guarding a bridge that was about to be demolished reported that a white man in khaki uniform tried to cross the bridge just before the fuse was lighted and told the Sikh that he was a British officer. The man's uniform was strange and his behaviour suspicious and the jemadar denied him permission to cross. The white man then tried to grapple with the Sikh and seize his tommy-gun. The Sikh shot him in the stomach. Japanese troops immediately opened fire from the far side and the Indians had to retire. This jemadar later received a decoration and the incident was mentioned in the official citation.

Some other Indian troops claimed to have surprised four white men in khaki uniform, definitely not our own men, in a locality up at the front that had been well penetrated by the Japanese. They were getting into a staff car. The Indians opened fire and killed two of the men but were not able to recover the bodies.

All these stories were told by Indians. Later one of the Argylls, a golf professional in civil life, claimed to have shot a white officer in enemy uniform with an armour-piercing rifle as he hastily took shelter behind a tree. The officer commanding the 11th Division told the correspondents one morning that it was an established fact that there were white officers with the enemy, not only observing operations but taking an active part in directing them.

No body was ever recovered and there is no concrete evidence to show that there were ever any European officers with the enemy. Nevertheless the cumulative effect of these stories was impressive and, when one considered the numbers of Germans who had filtered into all departments of the nation's life in Japan, it would not have been surprising if the Japanese had had Germans with them in Malaya. There must have been German military observers with the Japanese, probably some tank and aerial experts, and also a few German newspapermen. These Germans must have felt the tug of another loyalty when they saw the Japanese driving the white man out of Malaya, when they listened to the slogan 'Asia for the Asiatics' which has been the main

Japanese propaganda line throughout the war, and when they saw rich colonial lands like Malaya, French Indo-China, and the Indies, being taken away from beneath their eyes by the Japanese. They must have wondered sometimes whether this association with the Japanese was not a betrayal of another loyalty.

'Asia for the Asiatics'—was there ever a more absurd slogan? What is an Asiatic? Where does Asia begin and end? Yet there are Japanese who believe in it with the same woolly fervour with which a generation of Englishmen believed in 'the white man's burden'. And it makes an appeal in every eastern country to that small group which would sooner possess power with puppethood than no power at all.

13

THE FALL OF KUALA LUMPUR

About noon on January 8th we visited corps headquarters in
Kuala Lumpur and met one of those ineffably complacent and
incredibly stupid young staff officers who deservedly bring my
generation into disrepute. I had known him slightly in Japan
where he had occupied a junior position in one of the big oil companies. Here he was now, on the staff, having acquired a cap-
taincy and a moustache and all the stage mannerisms of the
British officer. That morning, he grudgingly admitted, there had
been just 'a spot of bother' up on the Slim River. Reports of 'the
battle' were just coming in. But the situation was 'quite well in
hand'. The spot of bother was perhaps the most decisive engagement fought on the mainland during the entire campaign. As a
result of it, all the British forces in north Malaya fell back upon
the Johore line, and the largest city on the mainland, Kuala
Lumpur, was occupied by the enemy with hardly a shot fired
within a radius of thirty miles from it.

The Japanese had surprised us by suddenly bringing up a force
of medium tanks. We knew they had the light two-men armoured
carriers but these twelve-tonners were a complete surprise. The
attack was launched in the early hours of the morning under
cover of darkness. Because of the prevailing obscurity it was difficult to establish exactly how many tanks took part. It appeared,
however, that at least six armoured carriers, twelve medium tanks,
and possibly some even heavier tanks, advancing in that order,
took part in the assault. Using an estate road, they came round our
advanced posts on the main road where we had anti-tank guns
ready, and joined the road some distance in the rear of the anti-
tank guns. They then advanced down the main road for several
miles, shelling and machine-gunning our men and their vehicles
and whatever else they could see. Then again they took to open
country and, after making a detour, attacked our positions on a

bridge over the Slim River. Fortunately one of our twenty-five pounders had got stuck on the bridge. Firing through open sights at point-blank range this gun succeeded in knocking out two and possibly three of the medium tanks. Shortly afterwards the tanks disappeared into a rubber estate up an estate road and did not put in an appearance again until they went into action against the Australians south of Muar about ten days later. According to the usual Japanese practice, the attack was accompanied by much waving of flags and shouting of 'Banzai'. The Japanese tanks wrought tremendous havoc. Our men and equipment were strung all along the road down which they rumbled with their guns blazing and with no artillery or anti-tank guns to stop them. They caused unspeakable confusion. They were closely followed by Japanese infantry who took advantage of the disorganization caused by the mechanized spearhead to fall ruthlessly upon our men. Losses were heavy, particularly amongst the Argylls and the Gurkhas. Fortunately, however, the attack was not pressed home as hard as it might have been. British forces from the rear succeeded in stabilizing the situation several miles south of the Slim River and the survivors of the units who had been so badly shot up were able to re-form again in the rear. A good many of the troops who had been cut off north of the Slim River succeeded in making their way back. Some came down the railway, some through the jungle, nearly all had to swim the river. A young gunner officer whom I met in Rasa had had two remarkable escapes. When the tanks first came down the road a shell from a tank cannon grazed his head but only touched it very lightly. During the course of his trek south he and his companion were surprised at one point by a camouflaged Japanese tank which promptly opened fire with a machine-gun at fifty yards range. A bullet went right through the heel of his boot without touching his foot. Worn and unshaven, he sat in the saddle of his motor-bike under the trees of the Malay village recounting his experiences. Another man we met there was a British planter from Kedah whose estate was overrun in the first few days of the war, since when he had been working with the army as an Intelligence and liaison officer. When the attack began he was with the Gurkhas and he had just brought a troop of them back with him from a point several miles north of the Slim River.

The Fall of Kuala Lumpur

The finest thing he had ever seen, he said, was the way in which those Ghurkas had stood up to that tank attack. Although it was dark and they could not see their targets clearly, although they were tired after many days of continuous fighting, although their rifles were useless against tanks, nevertheless the Gurkhas behaved like the trained and disciplined soldiers they were. They did not run or panic, but calmly took up positions at the side of the road and fired their rifles as best they could against the enemy.

The whole engagement was a débâcle. But it made our Command realize that this sort of thing could not continue. Another engagement of this nature and we would have no troops left in this north-western sector at all. Our men were bone-weary after over three weeks of non-stop heavy fighting. We were losing them at far too high a rate. The enemy kept on throwing fresh troops into the fighting. Now these tanks had come into action. If they had been effective on the estate roads north and south of the Slim River, they would be infinitely more so when operating on the numerous tarred roads that form a well-developed network all round Kuala Lumpur for many miles in every direction. But, even so, I think that, if our local Malayan command had been left to handle the situation, they would have lacked the strength of mind to order withdrawal on to the Johore line and would have continued this futile performance of trying to fight a delaying action with a tenth the number of men required to fight it successfully. Fortunately, General Wavell arrived at the front on the following day (Friday, January 9th), and the sensible, indeed the only, decision was taken. But it was a big decision. The entire British forces in north Malaya, the 9th Division from the east coast and the 11th Division (or what was left of it) from the west coast, were to fall back a distance of some 125 miles. A very small force was to seek to delay the enemy while the main bulk of the army withdrew. The next engagement of any magnitude after 'the spot of bother' on the Slim River was that fought at Gemas when the Australians first went into action.

The great move south began on Saturday morning. All Saturday and Sunday, all day and all night, the great withdrawal continued. An interminable convoy began to roll south. It was composed of all manner of vehicles. Large lorries filled with British troops, so dog-tired that they slept in spite of bumps and jolts. Civilian motor-cars commandeered by the military and hastily camouflaged by being spattered with mud. Lorries bearing the names of half the rubber estates in Malaya. Dispatch-riders darting in and out of the traffic on their motor-bicycles. Eleven steam-rollers belonging to the Public Works Department which had steamed all the way down from Kedah and Perak. Two fire-engines also making their way south. Enormous tractors used for clearing belted jungle trees in the construction of aerodromes, so broad that they took up most of the road, so heavy that their treads churned up the tarred surface. Low trollies towing sticks of heavy aerial bombs saved from the northern airfields for further use. Private motor-cars, from Austin 7's to Rolls-Royces, carrying Local Defence Volunteers, A.R.P. wardens, police officials. Camouflaged staff cars through whose windows one caught a glimpse of red tabs and hat-bands. Red Cross ambulances, ordnance vans, trucks fitted up with cranes and lathes and all equipment needed for field repairs. At intervals of about one mile there would be a lorry or car in the ditch, sometimes overturned, sometimes completely smashed up, sometimes burnt out and still smouldering. Light Aid Detachments, who did splendid work throughout the campaign and put hundreds of vehicles back on the roads, were at work on some of the cars which were only slightly damaged. These numerous smashes bore witness to frayed nerves, to tired drivers who had gone to sleep at the wheel or been suddenly dazzled in the black-out by oncoming headlights. When one reflected that most of the drivers had been driving almost continuously for the best part of the previous forty-eight hours, it was really amazing that there were not more accidents. The only casualty to be seen was a dead buffalo calf that had been knocked down and killed. Nobody bothered to get out and move it off the road and its mother stood on the grassy verge lowing in her puzzled distress. English, Scottish, Australian, Indian, Malay, Chinese drivers were at the wheels. Soot-blackened Tamils were keeping the steam-engines chugging along. When we came to a railway crossing, we saw one of the troop-trains proceeding south, filled with Indian troops. At another station there was a Red Cross train in the sidings, with its freight of pain and suffering. The trains were being

The Fall of Kuala Lumpur

driven by English and Australian drivers and fired sometimes by survivors from the *Prince of Wales* and the *Repulse*. (Nearly all the Indian engine-drivers returned to their homes when the war began. Their wages were meagre. There was little to induce them to stay and face the dangers of driving trains on the railway. Scratch European drivers were hastily recruited.)

In the villages and towns along the route Malays and Chinese and Indians stood in silent little groups, watching the long procession wind its way south. Neither pleasure nor malice nor sympathy were to be seen in their impassive countenances. Bewilderment was perhaps the emotion uppermost in their minds. Never before had warfare come to the Malayan peninsula. War was a phenomenon completely strange to these pacific, indolent, happy people. And now they saw the white *tuans*, who had always been in Malaya since they could first remember, heading for the south. In a few days' time another procession would wind its way through the village, also on its way south.

There was a book written about Malaya called, if I remember rightly, *Retreat from Glory*. The writer should have been in Malaya during this withdrawal. His title would have been truly *à propos*.

Fortunately the weather was cloudy during those two days of the withdrawal. If the Japanese had blown up one small bridge or begun to bomb the long procession, they might have caused appalling chaos. As it was there were practically no blockages or hold-ups on the road. The military police did a very good job of work in facilitating the withdrawal.

The Japanese must have marched into Kuala Lumpur on January 12th. Most of the previous morning and afternoon I spent in the city together with Til Durdin of the *New York Times*, Gilbert Mant of Reuter's, and Bill Knox of the *Sydney Daily Mirror*.

Most of the British forces in north Malaya had already passed through the city on their way south. There was still a small holding force some fifteen miles to the north. In the city itself demolition squads were blowing up the few remaining bridges. Indian sappers, with pneumatic drills, were boring into the road. The little boxes of white gelignite were stacked on the side. Occasionally there would be a loud explosion. One large iron bridge lay

112

A flight of Brewster Buffaloes

Air-raid damage in a street at Singapore

A Chinese A.R.P. Warden

Black smoke rising from burning
stocks of raw rubber

twisted and torn, with its girders in the river and the broken water main gushing its contents into the river too. On the outskirts of the city there were two or three high columns of black smoke—they had been a feature of Kuala Lumpur for several days past—as some remaining stocks of rubber were destroyed. We visited one such fire. The latex was burning fiercely, giving out such heat that one could not go within fifty yards, sending an enormous mushroom of inky smoke straight up into the air. The manager of this estate, an Australian who had been in Malaya for many years, had everything packed up in his car and was just about to leave for the south. The stocks of rice from the godown were being distributed to the Indian and Chinese labourers. Two Indian clerks were keeping a tally. It was quite orderly. Each labourer would have enough rice to keep him for at least two months. In the processing plant next door to the godown all the machinery had been smashed up. The old Chinese who for over twenty years had driven the engine that provided power for the plant seemed utterly bewildered. He himself had had to take a sledge-hammer and damage beyond repair those precious rods and valves and gadgets which he had oiled, greased, tended, watched like a father for so many years that he knew them better than his own children. The manager himself was heartbroken. He was a man who obviously took a tremendous pride in his work. It was the best estate, he told us, for miles around. Look at those young trees over there, never yet tapped, what beautiful condition they were in. He looked after his labour corps well and had never had any trouble with them. They were contented and worked hard. It was obvious that he hated having to leave all these people whom he had come to love, for whom he felt responsible. He was also having to leave his three Chinese servants. He could not take them and their numerous families down to Singapore with him. They would continue to live in the house and look after their master's possessions as long as they could.

The scene that met one's eyes in the city was fantastic. Civil authority had broken down. The European officials and residents had all evacuated. The white police officers had gone and most of the Indian and Malay constables had returned to their homes in the surrounding villages. There was looting in progress such as I have never seen before. Most of the big foreign department stores had already been whistled clean since the white personnel had gone. There was now a general sack of all shops and premises going on. The milling crowds in the streets were composed chiefly of Tamils, who were the poorest section of the population and therefore perhaps had the greater inducement to loot, but there was also a good sprinkling of Chinese and Malays. The streets were knee-deep in boxes and cardboard cartons and paper. Looters could be seen carrying every imaginable prize away with them. Here was one man with a Singer sewing-machine over his shoulder, there a Chinese with a long roll of linoleum tied on to the back of his bicycle, here two Tamils with a great sack of rice suspended from a pole, there a young Tamil struggling along with a great box of the best Norwegian sardines. Radios, rolls of cloth, tins of preserved foods, furniture, telephones, carpets, golf-clubs, there was every conceivable object being fiercely fought for and taken away. One man had even brought an ox-cart into town and was loading it up in the main street outside Whiteaways. The most striking sight I saw was a young Tamil coolie, naked except for a green loincloth, who had had tremendous luck. He had found a long cylindrical tin, three inches in diameter and a foot long, well wrapped up. What could it contain? Obviously a tin like this could only contain some rare and luxurious Western delicacy. He sat on the kerbstone turning the tin round in his hands. He wished that he could read that Western language so that he might know what the tin contained. Should he open it now or should he wait until he got home? Curiosity got the better of him and he decided to open the tin. Carefully he peeled off the paper and took off the lid. Three white Slazenger tennis-balls rolled slowly out, bounced on the pavement and then trickled into the gutter where they soon lost their speckless whiteness. Slowly an expression of the profoundest disappointment spread itself over the face of the young Tamil. He looked at the tin again, and then, with a gesture of supreme disgust, threw that too into the gutter. After a moment's thought he bestirred himself and moved off to see if he could find something more useful—a large roll of red velvet, perhaps, such as was even now being loaded on to a bullock-cart.

The only thing that was not being looted was booze. Several

days previously the army had collected as much of the liquor in Kuala Lumpur as it could find. Tens of thousands of bottles and cases were amassed. When the time came for a move south, Local Defence Volunteers laid into the cases of gin and whisky and other intoxicants with sledge-hammers and destroyed them. It was a wise precaution.

We went up to the Residency to see if the Resident was still there. It was a large spacious white house in park-like grounds filled with flowering trees, surrounded at a distance by other official residences. The place was deserted. The flag was down. There seemed to be no-one within miles. The big house was empty. It reminded me somehow of the *Marie Céleste*, that ship which was found in the South Atlantic sailing under full sail but without anyone on board and nothing to show what had happened. In the Residency a half-finished whisky-and-soda stood on the small table by the sofa in the drawing-room. Upstairs a woman's dress, half-ironed, lay on the ironing-table in one of the bedrooms. Two dispatches addressed to the Governor, typed out but unsigned, lay on the desk upstairs. In the offices on the ground floor the files were intact. The staff appeared to have downed pens in the middle of whatever they were doing and made off. A lorry, still in good order, was parked at the side of the building. Cases of beautiful silver ornaments, daggers of superb native workmanship, the presentations, doubtless, of Malay princes, lay in glass cases in the hall. The official portraits of the King and Quen smiled down from the walls. . . .

Those beautiful houses on the outskirts of Kuala Lumpur, those spacious mansions, with their lovely tropical gardens, where bougainvillaea and canna and hibiscus and many other flowering shrubs and creepers were in full bloom, were absolutely deserted, save perhaps for an old Chinese servant on the back premises or some dog whose master had not been able to take him south. At the hospital the Indian medical officer told us that all the European patients and staff had left for the south. He was in charge. The Majestic Hotel, which had remained open so long, thanks to the courage of the Chinese manager, one of those little men who in a crisis reveal unsuspected capacities for courage and strength, was closed at last. Indian sappers were preparing to demolish some of the buildings and sidings at the railway station. A club near Singapore, scene of fantastic scenes during the boom days in the rubber industry, was deserted. During an early raid on Singapore it received slight damage and was promptly evacuated by its beer-sodden secretary, one of the comparatively few men I met in Malaya who conformed to that picture of the 'whisky-swilling planter' about whom we have heard so much. The grounds in front of the club were laced with slit trenches and scarred by two or three small craters. The club in the good old days, with its atmosphere of affluent *bonhomie*, its gaily dressed women, its cricket and tennis on the lawn in front, its stingahs and pahits; the club in January 1942, deserted and derelict—the contrast was obvious, but it was moving. Some buildings just across the road had also been slightly scarred by bombs. The big clock in the clock-tower was smashed. (In that same tower the previous evening we had chased, with drawn revolvers, a fifth-columnist who was signalling with a flashing torch, but he heard us coming and escaped by another stairway.) The office of the Government Survey Department was boarded up and barricaded. We wondered how much they had taken with them when they moved south. The maps of Malaya, of many different kinds, large-scale and small-scale, published by the Survey Department, were superb productions. I threw a box through the large plate-glass window, smashed the glass, and climbed in. (All of us were in a reckless, truculent mood.) Not a thing had been removed. Motoring maps of Malaya, geological maps, forestry maps, maps of states, of districts, of villages, of islands off the coast, of rubber estates, maps of so large a scale that every tree was marked, lay there, tier upon tier, not in their hundreds but in their thousands. The Japanese undoubtedly had copies of many of these maps since they used to be on sale to the public. We know that they had excellent maps of the peninsula with them, or they would not have been able to use the terrain to such good advantage. But even so, it was difficult to see how all these maps could have been left behind for the enemy. I wanted to set fire to them. I wish now that I had done so. But one of my companions pointed out that it would also mean burning down the municipal buildings, several stories high covering several acres, and in a craven moment I desisted from starting such an enormous conflagration.

Meanwhile the milling crowds of looters in the streets seemed to be becoming larger. Men were coming in from miles around to see what they could bag. Others were coming in for second and third trips. Only in some areas did the Chinese shopkeepers, with that toughness of fibre which is the secret of their country's greatness, arm themselves with long wooden staves and band together to protect their property from the ravages of would-be despoilers. Such were the last hours of the largest city on the Malayan mainland.

14

THE AUSTRALIANS GO INTO ACTION

It is always difficult to write about Australian troops. They have certain obvious, rather irrelevant characteristics, which give them 'news-value' and render difficult a true appraisal of their quality as soldiers. We all know the legend of the lean, bronzed Digger from down-under, wild, undisciplined, unconventional, rip-snorting, and what not. It is a legend that I for one would like to see buried once and for all.

The two brigades of Australian troops in Malaya gave me the impression of being a body of serious-minded men, most of them married and a surprising number of them middle aged. Most of them had voluntarily left homes and good positions in order to go and do a job of work that they felt had to be done. They had been nearly a year in Malaya before they went into action. The period of waiting was not an easy one. They had volunteered for active service overseas and they found the inactivity of service in Malaya galling. Nevertheless they behaved with unexpected restraint and made themselves popular both with the native population and with the white residents. They were now in first-rate physical condition, morale was high, and they had a good understanding of jungle fighting.

Our command reckoned that after the withdrawal to Johore it would be some seventy-two hours before contact with the enemy was re-established. Actually it was well under seventy-two hours, so quickly did the Japanese follow up our withdrawal. They were engaged round Seremban by small bodies of Indian troops, but the first major clash took place in the afternoon of January 15th, exactly one week after the engagement on the Slim River.

Major-General Gordon Bennett, officer commanding the A.I.F. in Malaya, who had both his own Australians and (I believe) some other units now under his command, told me that, ever since he first arrived in Malaya, he had been impressed by the suitability of the terrain for ambushes. (At least, I believe he had some other units under his command. Even he sometimes did not seem to know very clearly whom he was commanding and whom he was not. There was a lot of switching about with commands. The 11th Division had three different commanders in the space of six weeks.) He resolved, in this opening engagement, to try and lead the Japanese into a trap. He chose a bridge on the main road a few miles north of Gemas. The bridge was prepared for demolition and a small group of men, upon whom would devolve the task of blowing it up, concealed themselves in the jungle near the bridge. One company took up positions in the jungle on each side of the road and behind them were strung out the rest of the battalion. The scheme was to let the Japanese through and then fall upon them from each side of the road. The men took up their positions and were given four days' rations. Only two days' rations would have sufficed, for the Japanese appeared very much earlier than we thought.

They cannot have expected anything at all. They came marching along the road about four in the afternoon of January 15th in small groups, many of them wheeling bicycles. Several companies came over the bridge and walked down the road blissfully unaware that keen eyes were watching them from out of the jungle on each side. The officer in charge of blowing up the bridge decided at last that he had let enough Japanese over. He waited until there were as many actually on the bridge as he thought there were likely to be at any one moment and then released the fuse. There was a tremendous explosion. The Japanese on the bridge were blown sky-high. Bridge, bodies, and bicycles went soaring up. The explosion was the signal for the battalion to fall upon the Japanese, which they did with loud yells. Rifles barked, tommy-guns sputtered, many of the Australians dashed in with their bayonets. Nearly all the Japanese who were on the hither side of the bridge were killed. Later it was estimated that between 800 and 1,000 of the enemy were killed, while the Australians suffered less than 100 killed and wounded. The Australians then fell back south of Segamat.

It was a triumphant beginning. It set all the Australians cocka-hoop. It had a tonic effect on all the British forces. But more was still to come.

Foiled in their attempt to come straight down the main road, the Japanese did what they always did and tried to come round the side. They switched their main push from Gemas to the coast. Bennett astutely foresaw what the probable Japanese strategy would be and took appropriate measures.

Our line along the south bank of the Muar river was originally held by the 45th Indian Brigade. It was a recently formed unit, the men were raw and untrained, and they had only been in the country a few days. When the Japanese attacked in the Muar river sector two days later, the Indians failed to hold them. The fighting was severe and several of the senior white officers of the brigade were killed. There was great confusion. When the 45th finally extricated themselves from the mess, they were sent back to Singapore and played little further part in the fighting. In an effort to stabilize the situation in the Muar sector, Bennett had to divert, first the 19th Battalion, and then the 29th, in the direction of the coast. The Australian anti-tank gunners went with them and took up a position nine miles south of Muar on the coast road. Bennett suspected that the Japanese might try to use their tanks down this coast road. He read the enemy's intentions correctly.

The 19th Battalion established contact with the enemy south of Muar late on the·afternoon of January 17th. Japanese units had filtered through the jungle. At dawn they launched an attack with tanks down the main road. They appear to have used only ten tanks, all of the medium type. Tank-traps had been constructed and two anti-tank guns, well concealed with thick foliage, were trained down the road, the first some distance ahead of the other. A point was chosen where the road ran through a cutting with banks on each side so that any tanks would have difficulty in turning there and would not be able to escape into the rubber plantations on each side. The tanks came rumbling down the road at dawn, each flying the pennant of the Rising Sun. The first gun allowed six tanks to pass down the road so that they could be dealt with by the gun in the rear, and it was actually the rear gun that was the first to go into action. The Australian gunners, tense with expectancy, waited until the leading tank was only fifty yards

away. Then, with loud shouts of 'Whacko!' they let the Japanese
have everything they'd got. The rear gun had a perfect field of
fire. Five tanks were picked off, one after the other. They tried to
turn round but could not do so in the cutting. Several caught fire
and the ammunition inside them began to explode. The sixth tank
was screened by the others and the gun could not sight it effec-
tively, so one of the Australians picked up two hand-grenades, ran
along the top of the cutting and threw them under the sixth tank,
putting it out of action. Most of the Japanese crews were killed
inside the tanks. A few scrambled out but were promptly picked
off by rifle-fire. Meanwhile the forward gun, further up the road,
had let loose against the four remaining tanks, which were also
close behind each other. They too were picked off, one after the
other. In this second engagement a remarkable incident is reported to have occurred. I give it for what it is worth, although I
was never able to obtain proper confirmation. A foreign officer in
uniform was reported by two of the Australian gunners to have
clambered out of one of the rearmost tanks, seized a bicycle that
was affixed to the rear of the tank, and pedalled madly off up the
road. If it was indeed a foreign officer, he could only have been one
of the German military experts who had been advising the
Japanese.

The correspondents at that time had erected their camp beds
and typewriters in a small villa on the outskirts of a town called
Kluang situated on the railway in central Johore. Hedley Metcalf,
a delightful Australian who was the official Ministry of Information photographer (now, alas, a prisoner in Java), was with the
Australian forces in the Muar sector, as also was the extremely
able and enterprising Australian photographic unit, consisting of
Jim Collins and Frank Bagnall, newsreel cameramen, and Cliff
Bottomley, still photographer. Hedley arrived on the scene shortly
after the tank engagement and took some of the few really good
pictures that were taken of the war in Malaya. The rest of us had
been up in the central sector all day and only heard about these
doings on the west coast when Hedley came in late that night. He
was greatly excited about it, and indeed it was a stirring tale as we
listened to it in that dimly lit room.

Hedley had had plenty of adventures that day. Japanese supporting infantry had followed up the tanks. After the tanks had been eliminated, the Japanese deployed into the surrounding country, which was mainly composed of rubber plantations. The Australians soon found themselves surrounded. Both sides began to snipe, the Japanese snipers resorting to the arboreal tactics which they loved so much. Both sides also brought their mortars into action. Colonel Robertson of the 19th Battalion was ambushed when coming up from the rear on the pillion of a dispatch-rider's motor-cycle. Both dispatch-rider and passenger were hit, and the machine crashed. Some fifteen minutes later a Bren-gun carrier dashed up from the rear and rescued both men. The dispatch-rider was already dead and the colonel died later, not from the bullet wound but from the injuries he had received when the motor-cycle crashed.

All day the Australians lay in the rubber, Hedley Metcalf with them. Sniping and the firing of mortars went on in desultory fashion. Japanese reconnaissance planes circled low overhead. The Australians dug shallow trenches for themselves. One Japanese sniper was concealed up a rubber tree only sixty yards away, but it was four hours before our men could pick him off. Armoured reinforcements could not come up from the south because the Japanese had felled a tree across the road. Late in the afternoon, however, the block was cleared, and Bren-gun carriers and armoured cars and other reinforcements came up to relieve the Australians. Hedley said that the feeling of relief when they heard the cars coming was so great that the men got up and cheered and shouted like madmen. Their casualties were slight, more being caused by the enemy's mortar-fire than by the sniping.

But the Australians in the Muar sector were not out of their troubles. The enemy began to redouble his pressure. A whole division of Imperial Guards, the very best ground troops the Japanese possess, were thrown into the fray in that area.

The men who had been engaged in the fighting on January 18th belonged to the 19th Battalion. The 29th Battalion was in the same sector but further to the east. The two units were not in direct touch except by wireless.

The 19th had a fairly quiet time on the night of January 18th although sniping went on intermittently all night. The following

The Australians Go into Action

day was also moderately quiet (except for the sniping) until about 4.0 p.m. when the enemy launched a heavy attack with infantry, strongly supported by mortar-fire and artillery. It was successfully repulsed, but at 5.30 the Australians decided to withdraw to make contact with the other battalion. Their mechanized transport was ambushed by Japanese machine-gun posts and had to be abandoned. Nevertheless the men succeeded in breaking through the encircling ring of Japanese troops, and fought for fifteen miles in the face of heavy fire before rejoining the 29th Battalion on the following morning. The two battalions, now united, received orders to withdraw to the east to our main positions in the central sector on the road north and south of Yong Peng. With them was Major Anderson, a most able British officer, transferred to the Australians as Brigade Major on January 15th. He was killed by shell fire at Muar and posthumously awarded the Victoria Cross.

Withdrawal to the east was complicated by the fact that the road from Muar to Yong Peng was blocked by machine-gun nests. The Australians attacked these nests with bayonets, routed the enemy, broke through the block, and advanced a considerable distance along the road with all the transport of the 29th Battalion. Then their way was blocked by a bridge that was in the hands of the Japanese, who were firing machine-guns from behind sandbags.

Early on January 21st the enemy launched an attack from the rear with infantry supported by dive-bombers, by mortars, and by at least one tank. The tank broke through and put much of the remaining Australian transport out of action, but did not damage, however, the wireless van or the ambulances. The Australians, who had collected some remnants of the 45th Indian Brigade, were now in a most serious position. They held half a mile of road and the jungle on either side. They were surrounded by the Japanese and their main line of retreat was blocked by the bridge. The tragedy of the situation was that the nearest British forces were only seven miles to the east.

That afternoon the ambulances with the worst cases of wounded and dying drove up to the bridge and permission was asked of the Japanese to let the ambulances through. The Japanese refused, and said that they would accept only the unconditional surrender of the entire force. The ambulances returned.

The Australians Go into Action

Attempts were made to relieve the beleaguered men. A guerrilla party of fifteen specially chosen men, armed with tommy-guns (the same men who had previously penetrated behind the Japanese lines and ambushed a car containing several high-ranking Japanese staff officers) was sent out from Bennett's headquarters north of Yong Peng with instructions to make their way through the jungle to the bridge and try to shoot up the Japanese machine-gunners there from the rear. The party never succeeded in reaching the bridge.

A counter-attack by British troops, including the Loyals, was planned for the next day (January 22nd) but, after being postponed three times, was eventually abandoned. (Why it was abandoned I never quite made out.) Early on the morning of that day food and supplies were dropped by aeroplanes on the Australians. At 11.5 Gordon Bennett sent Anderson the following message:

'Regret there is little prospect of any attack to help you. Special party, if successful, should have appeared before this. Twenty of your men and many Indians have already returned through the jungle to road which is at present in our possession. You may at your discretion leave wounded with volunteers, destroy heavy equipment and escape. Sorry unable help your heroic effort. Good luck.'

(The 'special party' was the band of fifteen picked men already referred to. The twenty Australians who had returned had been cut off in the early stages of the fighting, and the Indians were chiefly the remnants of the 45th Indian Brigade.)

Actually this message was never picked up as the batteries of the wireless van had petered out, but Anderson had given the same order that morning. The men began to make their way back. There was a track that led past a disused tin-mine which was fortunately not blocked by the Japanese and it was by this route that the survivors returned. At first it was thought that only very few would succeed in rejoining the main body of the A.I.F., but eventually some 650 men out of an estimated total of 1,600 for the two battalions made their way back.

This engagement fought by the men of the 19th and 29th

The Australians Go into Action

Battalions was a jungle epic. To appreciate the heroic nature of their exploit one must remember that they were under fire pretty continuously for six days, repelling enemy attacks, making counter-attacks, beleaguered by a numerically superior enemy, fired at by snipers concealed in the trees, bombed and machine-gunned from the air, pounded by mortar-fire. They got little sleep, for the sniping went on all night. There was never any thought of surrender. They kept their transport as long as they could. They did all they could for their many wounded, most of whose wounds had been caused not by snipers' bullets but by mortar shells and enemy bayonets. (Drugs ran out and the wounded suffered terribly.) They kept on attacking and counter-attacking. They maintained the offensive spirit right to the end. They showed what sort of fighters the men of the A.I.F. can be.

I met many of the survivors afterwards at Australian head-quarters. Grimy and unshaven, their clothes torn, their legs bleeding from scratches and insect-bites, they told me of their experiences as if it had all been part of the day's work. A small party of three who had been cut off in the earlier tank attack made their way through the jungle led by a Chinese. They swam across one river. A Malay ferried them across another. (I firmly believe that, despite what many people have said, the natives in Malaya helped us far more than they helped the enemy.) A young Digger, who looked as if he might be still in his teens, told me how he woke up one morning to find that his mate who slept beside him had been dead all night from a sniper's bullet. Yet another survivor recounted his experiences with such clarity and precision that he might have been dictating a letter to his steno-grapher in an office at home. A wireless operator told how wireless communication had been maintained right until the batteries failed, how the third man in the van was first wounded by mortar fire and then killed by a sniper. All the men who returned had stories like these to tell. One day, I hope, an Australian who took part in it will tell the tale. I can do no more than scratch the surface. It was a heroic engagement, and it achieved a most valuable objective. For five whole days these Australians stemmed the enemy's main coastal push.

The 8th Division fought with great distinction in Johore, despite the odds against them. If their record in Malaya had been based solely on their performances in Johore, it would stand very high indeed. Unfortunately a few of their units, those that had been brought up to strength with raw reinforcements from Australia, did not do so well in the fighting on Singapore Island. The strength of the Australian soldier, namely, his self-reliance and his conviction that *he* is the best judge of what action should be taken in any given situation, can also be his chief weakness.

The loss of Singapore was such a calamity, the Malayan campaign as a whole such a débâcle, that we are apt to forget the numerous acts of gallantry and fortitude which it produced, acts which were perhaps the more praiseworthy because they were performed in the teeth of such adverse circumstances.

And yet I sometimes wonder if a correspondent does not do a disservice to the general cause by recounting these tales of personal heroism which are so eagerly read by people at home. The tales are often so stirring that they clamour to be written, but, when things are going badly, do they not sometimes obscure the main issues?

I sent to my paper full reports of the three engagements referred to in this chapter: the ambush at Gemas, the destruction of ten Japanese tanks south of Muar, and the great fight put up by the Australians of the 19th and 29th Battalions on the road between Muar and Yong Peng. But the bleak fact remained that the Johore line had gone. In the minds of many observers (including myself) there was now nothing on earth that could save Singapore.

15

MEMORIES OF SOUTH MALAYA

The Imperial Guards whom the Japanese threw into the fighting in the Muar region represent the *élite* of the Japanese Army. They are not recruited from certain territorial areas as are the other divisions in the Japanese Army, but come from all over the country, and it is considered a great honour to be in this specially picked division, whose main responsibility it is to guard the Emperor's person. The men are of better quality than the ordinary Japanese soldier, and the officers are usually of good family.

I used to see them often in Tokyo, where they are usually stationed. They are easily recognizable. Whereas the cap-badge of the ordinary Japanese soldier consists of a five-pointed yellow star, in the case of the Guards the star is surrounded by a wreath. They are not necessarily the most fanatical soldiers in the Japanese Army. The fanatics come chiefly from the warm volcanic south, from Kyushu and western Japan. The Japanese who fought at Kota Bahru came from Kyushu. Nor are the Guards particularly renowned for their powers of endurance. When it comes to a long and arduous campaign it is the peasants from the cold northern provinces of the mainland and from the mountainous island of Hokkaido (which was my home for two years) who are most generally used. The Guards are chosen primarily for their loyalty and their reliability. When the 1st and 3rd regiments of the 1st Division (a Tokyo division), who were about to leave for Manchuria, staged their attempted *putsch* on February 26th 1936, it was the Guards who, together with other troops, gradually brought the insurgents to heel. In China the Guards were not used as shock troops, but two or three times they were thrown into the fighting when the Japanese High Command considered that a battle or campaign was reaching its climax.

There is no doubt that the morale of the Japanese troops in

Memories of South Malaya

Malaya was exceedingly high. Some of the Indian troops, when I asked them what they thought of the enemy, expressed the view that the Japanese were poor soldiers because they advanced often without taking cover and seemed to be courting death. There were many cases reported in which the Japanese advanced in open defiance of our fire. Their losses were often needlessly heavy. But of their spirit and push and their willingness to face fire, there can be no doubt. The war, of course, was a popular one with the Japanese Army, far more popular than the war in China. In China they had been up against some of the things that we were up against in Malaya—a more numerous enemy, who lived off the country and merged with the civil population, an enemy too who avoided frontal attack but loved to envelop and ambush the Japanese outposts. More was at stake in this war against Britain and America. For Japan it was victory or national suicide, and permanent relegation to the status of a third-class power. The prizes were richer. The spoils were the vast wealth of Malaya, the Philippines, the Indies, Burma. The satisfaction of racial animosity, the venting of an agelong inferiority complex in regard to the white races, gave spice to the whole undertaking. Besides, the Japanese forces had begun so phenomenally well. The campaign in Malaya was proving an absolute push-over. Nothing heightens the morale of an army so much as success.

The number of Japanese prisoners taken was not large, because we were on the retreat all the time. Those who were taken were treated well and were later sent to India. I remember two young Japanese who were caught in the Batu Pahat area where they had landed from sampans dressed as Chinese. They put on an act, but they only knew three words of Chinese and later they confessed that they were Japanese. Enemy prisoners were usually scared absolutely stiff, for they had all been taught to believe that if they were captured they would be shot out of hand. Soldiers are told in the Japanese Army that any prisoners captured by the enemy who are later released by the Japanese armed forces will be shot by the latter. In the Japanese military creed there is no such thing as surrender to the enemy.

The Chinese Army captured large numbers of Japanese prisoners during the war in China. Up in the north-west the communist

A Chinese bombed settlement on the outskirts of Singapore

Chinese carry on after a raid on Singapore

After an air-raid on Singapore

Chinese were the heaviest sufferers in the raids on Singapore

armies used to put the prisoners through a three-months' course in the errors of capitalistic imperialism and then send them back to preach the gospel of Marx amongst their comrades. Conversion was short-lived and very little preaching was done when the Japanese rejoined their units (as the Chinese well knew), but the wily Chinese found that, whereas previously the Japanese had fought desperately because they knew that death faced them anyway if they were captured, they did not fight with anything like the same fervour when they knew that surrender would only lead to a short post-graduate course in Yenan and subsequent release. There was an amazing film called *The Light of East Asia* made in Chungking with a cast composed entirely of Japanese prisoners of war who had consented to work with the Chinese. I met several of these young Japanese up in Chungking in the spring of 1941. They puzzled me a lot. Two or three told me that, although they knew that now they would never be able to return to Japan, they hoped one day after the war was over to go and live in Shanghai.

There is a sort of ancient shibboleth, which the Chinese will sometimes tell you, for distinguishing between Japanese and Chinese. If you capture an oriental and want to know if he is a Japanese or a Chinese, make him take off his socks. If his big toe is well separated from the other toes, he is a Japanese. He has been wearing *zori*, the sandals with a thong between the big and other toes. If his toes are like yours, he is a Chinese. Secondly, ask him to count with his fingers up to five. If he clenches his fist and then raises his fingers one after the other, starting with his little finger, he is a Chinese. If he starts with his palm open, and folds his fingers one after the other down into the palm of his hand starting with his little finger, he is a Japanese. Thirdly, there is one special word (which I forget unfortunately) which the Chinese can and the Japanese cannot pronounce. 'London Times' would be quite a good test, or any word with an 'l' in it, for nine Japanese out of ten would say 'Rondon Times'.

The belief was widely current amongst our men that the Japanese never took any prisoners. They certainly took some prisoners, for some of them escaped and made their way back to our lines. Three Australians who came back had been badly treated and made to work like ordinary coolies moving sacks of rice. They were given little food. On this subject generally there was little information available. There is no doubt that the Japanese are capable of brutalities. Their record in China shows that. There have been well-authenticated stories, not so much from Malaya, as from the Philippines and the Dutch East Indies, and we deceive ourselves if we try to pretend otherwise. The Japanese might also be expected to do what they could to humiliate their white captives in front of the Asiatic elements in the population in order to show that the white men are finished and they, the Japanese, are now the masters.

People often ask me how the Japanese treated their prisoners in Malaya and how they might be treating the tens of thousands of white prisoners whom they took at Singapore. Whatever the indications may be, there is not enough information available to the ordinary layman like myself for him to form an accurate opinion. Nevertheless, having lived in Japan for several years and having formed a high regard for some of the good qualities which the Japanese possess, I confess I should be sadly disappointed if I learned that their treatment of the captives at Singapore does not conform with accepted international usage and convention.

*　　　　　*　　　　　*

A few words on the Japanese Commander-in-Chief in Malaya, Lieutenant-General Tomoyuki Yamashita, might be of interest. He was one of Japan's foremost soldiers. He was once pointed out to me by a Japanese friend in Peking, a short, stocky figure, booted and spurred, with a long sword clanking at his side. If I had known what role he was going to play one day in the destinies of the British Empire, I should have paid closer attention. At that time, I believe, he was chief-of-staff to the Japanese forces in central China.

Yamashita was fifty-six years old when the Malayan campaign began. He had been born in the south of Shikoku, the smallest of the four main islands of Japan. In his military career he had had a long association with Germany. At one time he was Military Attaché to the Japanese Legation in Vienna, and later he studied military science in Germany. In December 1940 he was chosen, by reason of his ability as a soldier and his knowledge of German, to head a Japanese military mission to Germany and Italy. In Berlin he presented Brauchitsch, the Commander-in-Chief of the German Army, with an old *samurai* sword. He was also received by Hitler at the Chancellery. Interviewed afterwards by a Japanese journalist, he said that Hitler had told him that Japan should muster all her forces to establish a 'new order' in the Far East. To another Japanese journalist he said: 'I felt that in the mind of Hitler there was much spiritual matter transcending the material plane. Hitler said that since his boyhood he had been attracted by Japan. When he was a boy seventeen years old, he read carefully accounts of Japan's victory over Russia, and he was much impressed by Japan's astonishing strength.'

When the Sino-Japanese war broke out, he was a field commander in north China and saw much active service. Later he was made Inspector-General of the Japanese Air Forces.

Yamashita was a man who was absolutely up-to-date in the science and technique of war.

*   *   *

If the Japanese were throwing new troops into the battle, so were the British.

The best part of a division arrived at Singapore during the latter part of January. Amongst them was an East Anglian brigade, consisting of battalions of the Cambridgeshire, Suffolk, and Norfolk Regiments. We first met these reinforcements in the Ayer Hitam area. They arrived in Singapore (if I remember rightly) on a Monday, after a long ocean voyage. On the Thursday the Cambridgeshires and the Norfolks went up to the front to take up positions on the road between Batu Pahat and Ayer Hitam. On the Friday they were in the thick of it.

On the Friday morning a group of correspondents visited Brigade headquarters. Dive-bombers had been over constantly that morning. As we were studying maps with the Colonel there was suddenly a tremendous explosion. We immediately thought that the Japanese were bombing the headquarters. We flung ourselves to the ground. But nothing further happened, and there had been no whistle blown to signal the alert. There was no sound of aeroplane engines. Sheepishly we got up, wondering what had happened. It was one of our own twenty-five pounders ranging. There were two more shattering explosions before we left. I suppose our senses were more than usually alert after the dive-bombing which we had been through up-country. I noticed that my ears had become particularly sensitive and quick at hearing the noise of an approaching plane.

Those lads of the Norfolks and Cambridgeshires, with their fresh country voices—to men like myself who have had exactly two months in England during the last seven years, it was like a real bit of England suddenly dumped down in the middle of the Malayan jungle. Those newly arrived battalions put up a good fight. But circumstances were against them. They were plunged into the middle of this war after weeks at sea, unacclimatized to the tropical sun, their feet still soft. After four days they were in the thick of it, sniped at by infiltrating Japanese, bombed and machine-gunned from the air. Within a week of their arrival they were completely cut off in the Batu Pahat area. The Loyals and other units made unsuccessful counter-attacks to relieve them but eventually they had to be brought back to Singapore by sea. Naval patrol vessels used to slip up the coast by night, towing sampans and other small craft. The sampans would strike inshore up the creeks and bring away any men they could find. Rendezvous would be established and the next night the process would be repeated. It went on for about five nights until the Japanese had driven us back into the southernmost tip of the peninsula and controlled all the western coastline so that the patrol vessels could no longer operate.

This evacuation by the Navy was performed with skill and daring. It was a dramatic tale. It had 'news-value'. But the fact remained that we had lost many men in tragic circumstances, that the men who got back were tired and dispirited, that the Japanese were not only forcing us to fall back on the island but also gravely weakening the strength of those units on whom would devolve the task of defending the island. It was not alone the Norfolks and the Cambridgeshires. The same thing was happening to all the other units in Johore.

* * *

What enabled the Japanese to outflank us all down the west coast and frequently to threaten our positions and lines of communication inland was the constant use which they made of boats. Small launches, each towing ten or twelve barges filled with Japanese soldiers either in uniforms or native dress, would come down the coast at night. The launches would stop, the barges would make inshore and land anything from ten Japanese to twelve hundred. These would strike into the jungle, while the launches and barges, under cover of darkness, made north again, and repeated the process the following night. It was a form of operation that was extremely difficult to check or even observe. The men would lie quiet for perhaps two days, and then suddenly some trucks would be ambushed twenty miles behind our frontmost positions, or a large posse of Japanese would be found ensconced in an area that was believed to be clear of them, or a night attack would be made from the rear on some brigade or battalion headquarters. Over a thousand Japanese, for example, were discovered one day in a large jungle-covered hill to the south of Batu Pahat, the town where the headquarters of the East Anglian brigade was at first located. They had all come ashore in small boats.

*   *   *

The staff cars in which the correspondents drove about the countryside were driven by young Malay drivers of the Royal Army Service Corps. They were cheerful, happy-go-lucky young men. They would get a bit rattled when we were up at the front, but they worked very hard and loyally for us. The Malays of the 'Malay Regiment' did not distinguish themselves very greatly in the fighting, but some of the Malay ratings on vessels of the Malayan Navy behaved with the greatest courage and heroism in the face of enemy air attacks. As they had to stay on the boats they felt they might as well continue firing the guns.

The rulers of the Malay states usually disappeared into the jungle when war drew near their territories. Both in Kelantan and Perak the Japanese, immediately upon their arrival, appointed brothers of the Sultans to reign in their stead. The Sultan of Kelantan is reported to have returned to his capital after several weeks' hiding in the jungle and then to have found his younger brother riding round in a large car provided by the Japanese, flying a Japanese pennant on the bonnet. The new Sultan of Perak was a disappointed brother who had been passed over in the succession by the British.

One used to hear very different accounts of the behaviour of the native sections of the population, especially about the Tamils. Some men swore that they were the first to run when anything happened, others maintained that they had greater courage than either the Malays or the Chinese. I think the reactions of the native peoples depended in any given situation almost entirely on the leadership that was forthcoming. Left to follow their own instincts, Tamils would try to remove themselves as far from the scene of hostilities as they could. But if they had calm, tactful, and resolute leadership, they would behave with great fortitude. I met a young British official of the Posts and Telegraphs Department who was engaged on mending telephone wires behind the lines. When the Japanese bombed transport on the roads or attacked the railway, the explosions often cut all the telephone wires. The men under this young Britisher were all Tamils. He was full of praise for them. When they were first bombed, they were pretty scared and made off into the country. But, the second time, they took cover quietly and resumed their work when the planes went off. Now they were completely inured to these alarms. The truth was that in the young British official the Tamils had a leader whom they trusted and respected. Therefore they stuck to their work.

*   *   *

One evening at Kluang, when the Public Relations unit was based there, the unmistakable drone of a formation of bombers began to assail the ears of the correspondents. Whenever we heard the noise of planes, we used to assume automatically that they were enemy planes, until the contrary was proved. (It was rarely proved.) The drone became steadily louder. Only the previous evening three Japanese dive-bombers had suddenly appeared out of the sky and bombed Kluang, the nearest bomb falling about two hundred yards away from us. This evening there was no alert, and the drone was puzzling. Suddenly we saw the planes, twelve Wildebeestes, flying in formation. These biplanes flew so slowly that they gave the impression of being suspended motionless in mid-air. So incredibly ancient did their two wings look that we almost expected to see Orville Wright at the controls. Each had bombs fixed underneath its wings. They circled slowly round and then landed on the airfield. About 9.30 we heard them setting off in the darkness to drop their loads on the airfield at Kuala Lumpur and then return to Singapore. As one of their pilots told me 'the old kites are slow as a wet pig', but they were strongly built, could take an enormous amount of punishment, and carry a heavy bomb-load.

The following evening the Wildebeestes appeared again to land on Kluang airfield and make another raid on Kuala Lumpur. One's admiration for the pilots was mingled with indignation that we should be obliged to resort to the use of such outmoded machines against the enemy, such clandestine nocturnal tactics. That very day the Japanese had made their twenty-third daylight raid on Singapore, fifty-four fast modern twin-engined streamlined bombers flying high over the city.

Most of the Wildebeestes were lost in a daylight bombing attack on a convoy of Japanese transports and naval vessels off Endau, twenty miles to the north-west of Mersing on the east coast. A mixed force of Hudsons, Wildebeestes, Hurricanes, and Buffaloes (and also, I believe, some Wirraways) went up to attack the convoy. They were met by large numbers of land-based Japanese Navy 0's. Our losses were heavy and none of the Wildebeestes returned.

After I arrived in Java I heard that three days before the capitulation of Singapore an old Wildebeeste was seen flying over the Japanese positions in the west of the island doing what it could to bomb the enemy. If ever a man deserved a decoration, the pilot of that Wildebeeste deserved one.

*   *   *

In the early days of the war in Malaya a trip to the front was something of an undertaking. It would take one day by rail to reach P.R. rear headquarters, and then perhaps another day by car to reach the forward zone. We used to talk flippantly of the day when we should leave Singapore in the morning by car, drive up and have a look at the front line, and return to Singapore for lunch. This day came. I remember driving to see Bennett when A.I.F. headquarters, as well as corps headquarters, was in Johore Bahru, just across the Straits of Johore. I was anxious to check up on a story that the Japanese had been using gas and went with Captain Ferguson Stewart, who was the A.I.F. conducting officer. First we went to corps headquarters and had an interesting talk with Brigadier-General Fawcett, Brigadier of the General Staff, an able person who always talked very frankly to the Press. We came out and got into the car. Just as it was beginning to move I put my face to the window to look out and make sure that the skies were clear. It was an instinctive gesture, for up-country we could never hear planes above the noise of the car's engine and so had to depend entirely upon our eyes. It was as well I looked. Coming straight towards us, at an altitude of perhaps 15,000 feet, were twenty-seven Japanese bombers. We hurriedly ran the car under some trees, leaped out, and lay down in the ditch. Fifteen seconds later there was that shrill whistling which bombs make as they fall and then the loud rumbling roar as large numbers of them began to hit the ground. Fortunately none fell nearer to us than 150 yards. We were in a lucky spot. But they fell all over the little village of Johore Bahru which the Japanese knew was then our chief rear base of operations. (There was one good thing about these pattern bombings. They were unpleasant while they lasted, but they only lasted one minute and at the end of that time you were either dead or you were alive, and, if you were alive, you could get up and move about with perfect confidence. The dive-bombing was more unpleasant and the shelling was worse. When the dive-bomber flew away and you heard his engine no longer, you could relax. But the shell gave no warning at all and might appear out of the blue at any moment.) As we drove through the streets of Johore Bahru, there were big craters in the roads, telephone wires were down, a few buildings had been hit, and there was a thick black smoke, with an acrid burning smell, just beginning to clear away.

A.I.F. headquarters was on the far side of the town. We were told that Gordon Bennett was at an important conference upstairs.

I decided to wait. After ten minutes we could hear men coming down the stairs. Who should appear but General Wavell, together with all our senior military leaders, including Lieutenant-General Percival, Lieutenant-General Heath, and Major-General Bennett? I felt rather embarrassed. The local commanders looked at me vaguely disapprovingly as if they had intended the conference to be a highly secret one and were slightly displeased that the Press should have got on to the track of General Wavell. He, however, was very friendly and seemed to assume that I had come to see him. I suffered afterwards from terrible *esprit d'escalier*. There were so many questions that I might have asked General Wavell, but I was completely taken by surprise and felt rather embarrassed, and we chatted, if I remember rightly, about the Japanese air raids that morning.

The question that I should have liked to ask him was, 'Do you think we can hold Singapore?' I think that he would have replied in the affirmative because I think that he really believed that we could hold the place, not indefinitely perhaps, but certainly for two or three months.

I suspected at the time that the purpose of the conference was to decide whether we should push any more reinforcements into Singapore and try to hold it or whether we should virtually abandon its defence and withdraw as much equipment and as many troops as we could to Java.

*   *   *

One morning, when A.I.F. headquarters was at Rengam, I was talking to some Australians. They asked me what paper I was working for and what my name was. I told them. Then a young captain, addressing the other Australians, said, 'This man doesn't know it, but he's a cousin of mine.' It was my cousin Norman, whom I had never met before. He was one of the liaison officers on Bennett's staff and used to spend much of his time dashing about on a motor-bike.

Later he was taken prisoner at the time of Singapore's capitulation. My brother Alastair, who was in the British consulate at Peking, my other brother Colin who was a cadet in the colonial service at Hong Kong, my cousin Desmond, who was with the

A.I.F. in Amboyna, all are now in the hands of the Japanese. It is a large number of hostages for one family to have in enemy hands.

*　　　　*　　　　*

There was an action just north of Kluang where some Sikhs greatly distinguished themselves. I learned about it from one of the white officers who took part in the engagement. (Incidentally the white officers of these regular Indian units struck me as being very fine men on the whole. I suppose if you are in command of native troops you feel you have a moral responsibility to be tougher than the men under you, and braver, and calmer in the face of fire. If I were a regular soldier and could choose to enter whatever regiment I liked, I should choose without the slightest hesitation one of these Indian Army regiments, the Sikhs or the Gurkhas or the Dogras.)

On the afternoon of January 24th a Sikh battalion was sent north, together with a battery of British artillery, to stem the Japanese advance down the railway from Paloh to Kluang. They marched north, travelling parallel with the railway, by an estate road. At about dusk they were halted by a road block caused by a felled rubber tree and a party of Japanese opened fire from behind it. The leading company promptly deployed into the jungle on each side of the road. One platoon then crept round to the right to reach a small eminence from which they could fire at the Japanese with their rifles. Another platoon crept round to the left and charged the Japanese with their bayonets. Yelling at the tops of their voices, their fighting blood thoroughly aroused, the Sikhs fell upon the Japanese, and the latter, according to the young British officer, 'ran like rabbits'. The war-cries of the Sikhs and the squeals of the Japanese caused veritable pandemonium which only ended when the Japanese were either killed or had escaped.

That night the battalion camped in the jungle. Before daybreak a party of Japanese was sent to draw our fire, which it succeeded in doing. Having in this way located the position of the battalion, the Japanese brought their mortars into action. But we in turn located their positions and trained our own mortars and artillery on to them to such good effect that we not only silenced their mortars but again caused them to withdraw. There was also an exchange of small-arms fire but no more hand-to-hand fighting. When the Japanese withdrew they left behind them a large number of motor-bicycles and push-cycles, many rifles, mortars, and light machine-guns, and three pieces of light artillery. The Sikhs later tried to salve the light artillery, but they were fired upon, and gave up the attempt. The battalion commander said that he actually counted 137 Japanese dead, and their total casualties must have been very much greater. Our casualties were not heavy.

The Sikhs were eventually obliged to withdraw down the railway, but at least they had succeeded in causing substantial damage to the enemy and had delayed his advance on Kluang. They came back tremendously pleased with themselves after this successful little encounter with the enemy.

I can well imagine that nothing is more calculated to put fear into a Japanese than the spectacle of an enormous bearded and turbaned Sikh descending upon him with his bayonet, yelling like mad.

*   *   *

Another story which occurs to me is that of a party of sixty men, half of them Indians, half Australians, who were cut off in the Muar region. They rejoined their units after a four-day trek through jungle, swamp, and rubber plantations. Some of the survivors told me that they owed their return solely to the native inhabitants. The Malays provided guides through the jungle and the Chinese in the villages fed them and looked after them. At one place Chinese villagers quite spontaneously produced food, which consisted chiefly of rice, dried fish, and China tea, for the entire body of sixty men. To feed as large a body of men as that is no mean undertaking when you consider how poor are these Chinese labourers who work on the rubber estates, how precious their stocks of food must be to them.

On the east coast the Australians once caught two Japanese entirely owing to the co-operation of the Malays, who reported the arrival of these strange people and later guided the Australians to them. The Japanese were believed to have been dropped by parachute. They were wearing Malay dress and could speak a little

Malay. But they still insisted upon carrying, wrapped up in cloth, their long two-handed ancestral swords. It was these swords which first made the Malays suspicious. Their khaki uniforms they carried tied up in a small bundle.

It is not true to say about the Malayan campaign that the native population was on the side of the Japanese. There was a very small minority working actively with the enemy. The vast majority felt that the conflict did not particularly concern them. When it drew near to them, they would try to get as far away from it as they could. But there were also many instances where the natives displayed their sympathy with, and actively assisted, those white people who had been in their country so long.

* * *

There is not very much to say about the progress of the war in Johore. Less than two weeks after the Australians first went into action against the Japanese we were all back on Singapore Island, with the causeway blown up and the island's link with the mainland destroyed. Once our forces failed to hold the Japanese in the northern part of Johore, our command decided not to contest too fiercely the Japanese advance down the southern part of Johore but to fall back on the island with units as intact as possible and to conserve strength for the siege. Few of the units, of course, fell back intact, and many were badly cut up in the fighting in the southern regions of the peninsula.

It is not just to blame the Indians who gave way on the Muar River for what happened subsequently. If the Japanese had not outflanked us on the coastal sector, they would have outflanked us on the sector east of the Yong Peng–Ayer Hitam road in the centre of the peninsula. When we talk loosely about 'the Johore line', we are referring, strictly speaking, to a certain area in north Johore where, if we had had enough properly trained and equipped fighting men, we could have exploited the terrain to sufficient advantage to check the Japanese advance. There were never enough men. The Australians were fresh, were well trained and properly equipped. But there were only two brigades of them. If there had been two divisions of them, if, moreover, there had been three squadrons of Hurricanes operating with them, the whole story might have been different. The other British troops in Johore, who outnumbered the Australians by perhaps three to one, were either tired troops who had fought their way down the greater part of the peninsula, or they were fresh reinforcements completely new to the country and the sort of fighting they were called upon to do. Given the balance of opposing factors that prevailed just before the main battle was joined in southern Malaya, I am convinced that the outcome would have been the same no matter how brilliant the generalship might have been.

16

THE SIEGE BEGINS

When my wife left Singapore for Batavia in the middle of January, I went to live in the Po Leung Kuk Home, universally referred to in Singapore as the Home for Fallen Women. Admittedly the translation of the Chinese characters reads 'Virtue Protection Bureau', but the Home was primarily an orphanage run by the Chinese Secretariat. The inmates were nearly all young Chinese girls who had been ill-treated or abandoned by their parents, children whose cases had come up in the courts. Only a few had been rescued from brothels. When the air raids began on Singapore and there was danger of bombing and fire, the Secretary for Chinese Affairs was anxious that there should be one or two men on the premises, and some of the young men in his department, who had been forced by the army to evacuate their houses on the western side of the island, went to live in the Chinese matron's house in the Home, while the matron, who was called Clara, moved to one of the other buildings. My special friend there was a young British official who was in the Labour department of the Chinese Secretariat. It was an excellent place to live, for not only was it right in the middle of one of the Chinese quarters but I used to hear from my friends, who were dealing with the Chinese all day (and, may I add, dealing with them very capably?) all the gossip that was circulating among the Asiatic sections of the population now that we were all living under siege conditions.

The siege began officially about eight o'clock on the morning of Saturday, January 31st. At that hour there was a loud explosion, which we could hear clearly on the south side of the island, as the Johore causeway was blown up. Soldiers who witnessed the demolition told me how road, rails, water mains, lock-gates, all went flying sky-high. Not long afterwards a party of correspondents drove to the north side of the island to have a look at what had been done. At the far end of the causeway there was a breach some thirty yards wide through which the water was pouring, for the water on one side of the causeway, curiously enough, was higher than on the other, and there was quite an elaborate lock to regulate the flow. The lock was completely destroyed. All down the causeway on the hither side of the breach there were coils of barbed wire. Some light guns were trained down the causeway from this end.

According to Japanese reports, the Japanese contrived to fill the breach shortly after the assault on the island, presumably with the use of pontoons, and their tanks came charging along the causeway and reached the island where they played a big part in the fighting. Many people have asked why the causeway was not properly destroyed. The truth is that the causeway was not a particularly easy thing to destroy. It was not a bridge or a viaduct. It was a long straight stretch of concrete road (1,100 yards long and 40 yards broad) built on a foundation of enormous boulders weighing five and ten tons. It had taken several years to build and had cost £4,000,000. To blow up the entire length of such a massive structure would have required several tons of dynamite. In any case I think the argument about the demolition of the causeway is somewhat irrelevant. The Japanese had not only landed on the north-western coast, but had already occupied the western half of the island, before they began to repair the breach in the causeway. If they had wanted to do so they could have quite easily landed their tanks from barges as they have done sometimes in the war in China.

How narrow were the straits may be gauged from the fact that some soldiers that morning, who had been on the further side when the causeway was blown, swam the straits with ease. Many more, who had been cut off in Johore, were to swim their way back during the next two or three days.

We sat in a coco-nut plantation down by the shore of the straits and from the cover of some bushes looked across to the mainland. For the first time in this campaign there existed what might accurately be described as a 'front' or a 'line'. It was one of those perfect tropical mornings that one used to get in Malaya, a sky of exquisite pale blue, clouds of a fleecy whiteness. A light breeze was blowing up the straits from the east and the water lapped gently against the boulders of the causeway. So clear was the atmosphere that the buildings on the further shore could be picked out in smallest detail. The most conspicuous buildings were the recently finished Johore government offices, in which an attempt, not unsuccessful, had been made to combine modern concrete technique with Islamic design. The crescent and star of Islam caught the rays of a sun that was still low in the heavens. (The building was later badly scarred by our twenty-five pounders, for the enemy began to use the tower as an artillery observation post.) Further to the west rose the central dome and the four surrounding minarets of the mosque. Behind it was the royal park where the discipline of an English garden had been blended with the wild luxuriance of the trees and plants and shrubs of the tropics to form an altogether unique and lovely pleasaunce. The old palace, where one of the last of the true oriental despotisms had held sway, could be dimly descried through the trees of the park. Of what magnificent entertainments, on a lavish Eastern scale, had it not been the scene! Still further to the west was the big modern red-brick hospital, now evacuated of all the British wounded who had been placed there. And then there stretched a long low vista of mangrove swamp and shrub, with, in the distant background, the hills from which had come Singapore's water supply. The Sultan's palaces, however, were empty. The old man had retired to one of his residences further inland. A week previously he had sent his Roumanian wife to Singapore so that she should be evacuated with the rest of the white women. But then his heart had failed him, he pleaded with her to return, and she was now with him. Gordon Bennett was one of his few friends who went to say good-bye to him. He said that Sir Ibrahim was extremely depressed and thoroughly fed up with the British and everyone else. Whatever else he may have been, the Sultan of Johore was a brave man, who in his younger days used to go tiger-hunting on foot, an able financier, who had raised his little kingdom from bankruptcy to affluence, and a picturesque figure, one of the last of the Eastern potentates, who did much to give colour to a drab and ordinary world.

As one gazed across the Straits of Johore that morning, one

Japanese tanks destroyed by the Australians
south of Muar

The Australians get another Japanese tank
in Malaya

Tanks destroyed by Australians at a road block

could not help thinking that Japanese officers were probably doing the same thing from the further shore. What thoughts can have been in *their* minds as, from the cover of shrubs and bushes, they gazed through their field-glasses at the low-lying green expanse of the island of Singapore, this richest prize in the whole of south-west Asia? From Johore village they could probably see, above the swamps and the rubber and palm plantations, the giant crane of the Naval Base, the masts of the Admiralty transmitting station, and a great column of black smoke from some oil tanks which their bombers had set on fire the previous day.

Also in the coco-nut plantation were some men operating one of the searchlights down on the shore which were supposed to light up any Japanese attempts to land in barges or small boats by night. They had a few sandbags to protect them but there was no concrete fortification. Perhaps it is difficult to operate a searchlight from a pill-box. I don't know. They described themselves accurately, but fairly cheerfully, as a suicide-squad. By day they concealed themselves in a three-foot deep rifle-pit. Snipers' bullets whined overhead occasionally.

The siege of Singapore had begun. But we were not allowed to describe it as a siege. There was a comic episode that evening. Each evening at 4.30 there was a Press conference at which the official communiqué would be handed to the correspondents. A military spokesman would answer any questions and give us any background material that was available. It is the misfortune of correspondents in wartime that most of the officers appointed to deal with them are men who are physically or intellectually unfit for active service. The Singapore military spokesman was there because he had broken his leg. (This is no criticism of the officer in question, who was a charming person and did his best, but he was not adapted to the job.) The question arose that evening whether we might use the word 'siege' in our messages. The spokesman, however, would not permit us to use this word, because, he said, it would have a depressing effect on local morale. In vain did we protest and assure him that every newspaper and broadcast in the world would soon be saying that 'the siege of Singapore' had begun. The spokesman stuck to his point. We might say that Singapore was 'besieged' but we were not to use the word 'siege'. I pointed out that it was inconsistent to permit us the use of a certain English verb but to deny us the use of the noun which is cognate with that verb, for possible ill effects which that English noun might have on a population whose native tongue was not English. The spokesman was immovable. So it seemed to me that the only thing to do was to make sure that a sensible word was substituted in our messages for the word 'siege' which we had all used. It was eventually agreed that the horrid word 'investment' should be substituted. But something went wrong in the censorship and when I looked at my messages in the morning to see how they had been treated by the censor I found that the word 'siege' had been excised and the incredible word 'besiegement' substituted. It is a word that is not even to be found in the English dictionary. Sub-editors in *The Times* office must have thought that their Singapore correspondent was suffering from shell-shock when they received a message beginning: 'The besiegement of Singapore began officially at 8.0 this morning.'

It is perhaps worth noting in passing that the military spokesman at the conference three evenings later gave it as his personal opinion that the Japanese would not attempt to attack Singapore at all, but would bypass it and strike at other objectives. Later, there were people in Java who thought that the Japanese would not strike at Java. Now there are people in Australia who think that the Japanese will not strike at Australia.

There was a comic exchange with the censors which took place about this time. Harold Guard was hard up for something to write about one afternoon and so he wrote a homely little story describing wartime conditions in besieged Singapore, how he had had to do his own washing that morning in his bombed house, how he had gone out and bought a leg of pork for his lunch and cooked it himself, and so forth. It was a story not without interest to millions of housewives. The censors, when they came to read the message, could not understand how anyone could possibly be interested in reading about a leg of pork at such a juncture. They passed the message on to Military Intelligence who scrutinized it carefully. A leg of pork. Most mysterious. Eventually they came to the conclusion that this seemingly innocuous message was really an elaborate code, the leg of pork referring perhaps to some of our defences which were in the shape of a leg of pork. Harold was ordered up to Fort Canning and closely interrogated. He was prohibited from sending any messages at all. In vain he protested. It required the personal intervention of Rob Scott, head of the Ministry of Information, to extricate him from this difficulty and absolve him from the charge of being a fifth-columnist.

There was considerable friction between correspondents and censors at the beginning of the campaign. There always is this friction in time of war. I think it is a good thing. It means that both parties are on their toes. After a few weeks the whole Press Relations organization improved enormously and towards the end it was beginning to work very well. There were times when I felt that I was the victim of stupidity, or, usually, inconsistency, on the part of the censors, but on the whole I do not think that the correspondents, once the war had got well under way, were debarred from presenting a moderately accurate picture of what was happening in Malaya.

When the causeway was blown up, the water mains which brought most of Singapore's water supply from the reservoirs in Johore were also destroyed. Water, however, was not a serious problem. There were two reservoirs on the island and at the time of the siege they were brimming full. Water was being rationed, not by turning the water off between certain hours, but by making three or four households use the same tap. Water was thus available at any time although for most houses it had to be fetched in buckets. Baths became something of a luxury.

Nor was food a problem. If the Japanese had cared to bypass Singapore and try to starve the island into surrender, it could have held out for months. The Food Controller, on whom I paid a visit when the siege began, told me that the last pig census revealed that there were 125,000 pigs on the island at the end of December. I could hardly believe the figures. There was enough food of all sorts for at least six months. There was actually too much flour. The Food Controller said that if I could arrange to have several thousand tons of flour shipped to Ceylon he would gladly ship it there. Every ship coming in to Singapore had been bringing in flour. Rice, not flour, was the main diet of the population. But there was plenty of rice also. Several air-conditioned cinemas had been taken over by the Government and were being used for storing supplies of food.

There was little rationing in Singapore. Hotels and restaurants were supposed to observe two meatless days weekly, but one hardly noticed this restriction as game and poultry were not counted as meat. Fresh fruit, vegetables, and eggs were the only materials which became at all scarce. There was abundance of tinned fruit and vegetables and each person was allowed two tins a day. There was no rationing of sugar and milk, and the allowances both of meat and butter were three or four times what they are in England. There seemed to be no shortage of liquor.

On January 31st General Percival issued an order of the day which I shall quote:

'Our task is to hold this fortress until help can come, as assuredly it will come; this we are determined to do.

'Any of the enemy who sets foot in our fortress must be dealt with immediately.

'The enemy within our gates must be ruthlessly weeded out. There must be no more loose talk and rumour-mongering.

'Our duty is clear. With firm resolve and fixed determination we shall win through.

'For nearly two months our troops have fought an enemy on the mainland who has had the advantage of great air superiority and considerable freedom of movement by sea.

'Our task has been to impose losses on the enemy and gain time to enable the forces of the Allies to be concentrated for this struggle in the Far East.

'To-day we stand beleaguered in our island fortress.'

On February 5th there was an order of the day by General Wavell which I shall also quote:

'Our part is to gain time for the great reinforcements which we and our American allies are sending to the Eastern theatre.

'We are in a similar position to the original British Expedition-

148

ary Force which stopped the Germans and saved Europe in the
First Battle of Ypres.

'We must be worthy successors to them and save Asia by fighting these Japanese.

'We have now reached an area where we cannot be constantly
outflanked and where the enemy cannot exploit superior mobility.

'We must yield no strip of ground without fighting hard, and
must leave nothing behind undestroyed that would be of the least
service to the enemy.

'Our friends and allies, the Dutch, are carrying out this policy
in every part of the Indies with sacrifice and resolution.

'I look to you all to fight this battle without further thought of
retreat, and to make the defence of Singapore as memorable and
successful an exploit as the defence of Tobruk which British,
Australian, and Indian troops held so long and so gallantly.'

One of the minor lessons of the war in Malaya is the folly of
public pronouncements unless the speaker really has something to
say. It has become the fashion to celebrate any event or any
appointment with stereotyped exhortatory or congratulatory telegrams. I cannot believe that they have any effect. Afterwards they
tend to react on reputations.

Two or three days later I made a trip out to the Naval Base with
Rob Scott and Henry Stokes. It is my most tragic memory of the
whole Malayan campaign. There were some Indian sentries at the
gate but they did not bother to ask us what we wanted. The
barrack-like buildings just inside the gate which used to house
part of the labour corps of 12,000 Asiatics were completely
deserted. A little further on were the headquarters of the Naval
Base police, who had been disbanded several days previously. An
area of one acre outside the office was knee-deep in their uniforms.
Shirts, turbans, truncheons, gas masks, leather belts, wooden
lockers, were lying about in a wild mess. I don't know what can
have happened. It was so unlike the Navy to tolerate mess of any
sort. We later salvaged fifty of the gas masks as we knew there
were hospitals in Singapore that had none at all. We parked the
car and walked to the crest of a ridge to look down upon the base.
There were few signs of human activity. Occasionally a lorry

would speed down to the godowns near the shore where they were still trying to salvage some of the stores. The Japanese had already begun using their mortars from the far side, and one suspected that these lorry-drivers were slightly nervous, by the speed with which they raced along. Over to the left there were twenty huge cylindrical oil-tanks. Four were on fire. A strong breeze was fanning the flames and scattering the smoke. They had been burning for three days. At night from my bedroom window I could see a red glow in the sky to the north-east. We wondered why the other tanks did not catch fire. Three Japanese reconnaissance planes were circling round in the clouds over the Straits, picking out our positions and spotting for the enemy artillery. Round and round they flew, sometimes disappearing into the clouds, sometimes coming so directly over us that we took cover for a few minutes. Once or twice they flew sufficiently far inland over the island for the Bofor guns to take a long shot at them. We walked through the various machine shops and storehouses. Here were the great furnaces where huge blocks of iron and steel could be forged and rolled, enormous hydraulic presses, vast troughs into which the molten metal was poured. Here were lathes of many types. (The Australian Government Commissioner tried to have some of them removed so that they could be sent to Australia. If they were worth thousands of pounds when they were bought in peacetime, they were now priceless, for they were no longer obtainable. But most of the equipment was too heavy and had to be left, despite the tireless efforts of Wootton, the Assistant Commissioner, and other British volunteers who toiled day and night with him.) Here was the huge boiler-shop, with great boilers still there. A mortar shell had come through the roof and torn the roof open, but otherwise had done little damage. Here was the storeroom for aeronautical equipment, spare floats for seaplanes, propellers, struts, pieces of fuselage and wing. Here was the storeroom for wireless equipment, rows and rows of shelves with every conceivable form of wireless device and gadget. Stacked on the floor were hundreds of boxes of those large electric bulbs used in radio work. Towering up into the sky over the storerooms and machine-shops was the great crane which could lift an entire gun-turret out of a battleship. A mortar shell had scarred slightly one of its girders. The three of us strolled, with a foolish bravado, along the waterfront in full view of the enemy on the further side of the straits. They picked us up pretty quickly and a mortar shell landed with a resounding thwack fifty yards behind us. After that we took cover and kept behind buildings as far as we could. Just off-shore was the floating-dock, its upper works protruding above the surface of the water, the great floating-dock which could accommodate a 45,000-ton battleship, towed all the way out from England by Dutch tugs. It had been dynamited, but I imagine that a floating-dock, like a causeway, is a difficult thing to destroy completely. We came across a party of English soldiers under a sergeant. They had some machine-guns down on the shore. Some concrete slabs gave them a little protection against rifle-fire from the further shore, but they had no protection from the air. There was plenty of barbed wire on the shore but not much else. From one of the godowns near the foreshore naval ratings were loading supplies of food, mostly boxes of tinned goods, on to two lorries. We struck inland up another long line of storehouses. One was filled with huge coils of rope and hawser and wire and cord. A couple more mortar shells exploded down near the front where we had left the soldiers. We came to a cross-roads where the enemy had evidently trained one of his mortars. It was pitted with five small craters. The fire had been pretty accurate. The little villas where the officers and their wives used to live were completely deserted. In peacetime these rows of villas used to remind one of a street in Surbiton or any English suburb. At the petty officers' mess there were three dartboards stacked just inside the entrance. In one of the rooms there was an unfinished meal on the table. From the police mess we took three crested china beer mugs. As further mementoes of this expedition I remember taking home a coil of cord (for what reason I do not know) and the head of a two-inch mortar shell. The Administration buildings lay in an enclosure that was surrounded by an iron palisade topped with spikes. The gate to it was barred but a shell had made a hole in the palisade and we climbed through it. The Administration buildings formed a sort of *sanctum sanctorum*, a holy of holies. In peacetime, once you had penetrated into the Naval Base, which was hard enough if you did not have the requisite pass, you still had to go through careful scrutiny before you could reach the Administration buildings. They were completely deserted. Empty were the wooden mat-sheds where the Commander-in-Chief, Far East, and his staff, used to have their offices. No less empty were the concrete buildings behind. They had housed the Commander-in-Chief of the China Squadron, his numerous staff, Far East Combined Intelligence Bureau, and many other bodies. This was the brain-centre and the nerve-centre, not only of the Navy but of the entire British fighting organization in the Far East. We went upstairs into the Commander-in-Chief's office. It was in this room that Rob Scott first introduced me to Sir Geoffrey Layton. Perhaps it was in this very room that had been held that fateful conference which decided whether the *Prince of Wales* and the *Repulse* were to remain in Singapore or to proceed up the coast towards the Gulf of Siam. Now it was completely bare, save for a large naval map of the world strung along one of the walls and some miscellaneous 1941 year-books, *Whitaker's Almanack* and *Who's Who*. Mortar shells had hit the building and burst a water-pipe which was flooding the lavatories. Everything had been removed except desks and chairs. We left the building, climbed out through the gap in the palisade, walked back to the car, and drove away. The Indian sentries at the gate hardly seemed to notice us.

We drove to the neighbouring airfield at Seletar. The aerial base at Seletar was supposed to be equivalent to, and complementary to, the Naval Base. It had indeed taken a tremendous hammering. Day after day, huge formations of Japanese bombers had come over and bombed it. The craters there were the biggest that I saw on Singapore. Hardly a building stood intact. Most were blackened skeletons. The field itself was pitted with bomb-holes. It was littered with some half-dozen burnt-out Hurricanes and Buffaloes and Blenheims. In some of the less-badly damaged hangars near the shore were aeroplane engines still in crates and much miscellaneous aeronautical equipment. The place was deserted except for some English soldiers down on the foreshore. They had three or four machine-guns, not many, which had been emplaced amongst some rocks. There were coils of barbed wire down by the water's edge. It seemed to Rob and myself that there were ludicrously few men in that particular sector, and those that were there, we thought, might have been very much more active than they were in preparing positions. The Singapore Yacht Club was located there. Yachts with engines were moored off-shore. Others were pulled up on the beach under mat-sheds. We drove off round the field, past all those burnt-out buildings, out at the gate, and then home.

How much of the plant and equipment that we saw at the Naval Base was eventually destroyed I do not know. The Navy had left the work of demolition to the Army. I should not be surprised if much valuable equipment fell into the hands of the enemy. The demolition at Seletar, wrought for us by the Japanese air force, was all too tragically thorough.

The great Singapore Naval Base, which had been twenty years a-building and had cost us £60,000,000, had become simply one military sector out of many such sectors in the defence scheme of Singapore. It had been built to harbour a grand fleet. For less than a week it had given shelter to two British battleships, and then they had sailed out, never to return. It had been built on the northern shore of the island so as to be furthest away from the shells of the enemy. It was now in the very front line, and two-inch mortar shells were being lobbed on to it from the other side of the straits. The huge naval guns which protected it pointed out to sea. They were embedded in concrete and could not be turned to point inland. Most of them were never fired. People had sheltered, not behind the Naval Base, but behind the defensive concept of which the Base was the chief visible expression. Other people had done the same thing behind the Maginot Line.

We could not help feeling that afternoon that we were witnesses to one of the supreme tragedies of this war.

17

THE MEN AT THE TOP

Singapore was crying out for leadership.

There was a good deal of defeatism about, especially amongst the British. During the previous two weeks the Government had evacuated most of the British women and children. The reinforcements of ships and planes which, we hoped at the start of the war, would realize Singapore's potentialities, had arrived too late and in insufficient quantities. The battle of Johore, which many of us regarded as the battle of Singapore, had been fought and lost. Mr. Churchill had said in the House of Commons, *à propos* of the Far East, that he might soon have very much worse news to tell his listeners, and this was interpreted by most people as referring to the loss of Singapore. The leading daily paper, the *Straits Times*, which was owned by, and represented the views of, vested interests, was doing everything it could to undermine people's faith in the local government, doing it doubtless with the best intentions. It had always been splenetically hostile to the local government and the Malayan Civil Service. Earlier it had advocated the appointment of Mr. Duff Cooper as Dictator of Singapore, with plenary powers, for the duration of the crisis. While its long editorial tirades might have served some purpose in times of peace, they did a great disservice now by still further weakening public confidence in the only civil authority that existed. There were many amongst the British who thought that we could not hold Singapore. There were others who thought that we did not intend to hold it. There was little confidence either in the civil government or in the military command.

There was also considerable defeatism amongst the troops. During the long retreat, often a bloody retreat, down the mainland, the army had acquired the psychology of retreat. General MacArthur said at a Press conference, after he arrived in Australia, 'Men will not fight, and men will not die, unless they know

154

what they are fighting and dying for'. Amongst the tens of thousands of British troops on Singapore Island, probably only the Australians could have answered adequately the question 'What are you fighting for?' They did feel, in a vague way, that they were fighting for Australia and for their homes and families. London Cockneys and Scottish peasants could be forgiven if they failed to see that Malaya, with its Asiatic inhabitants' who appeared to care so little whether they were governed by the British or the Japanese, with its tin mines and rubber plantations which enriched still further a few already rich men but did little to make life tolerable for them, was a stake worth dying for.

Considering what morale was like among the British, it was surprising that morale among the Asiatics was not very much worse than it was. They took their cue from the white people and were quick at detecting what the prevailing thoughts and emotions were among us. Labour was proving an increasingly grave and difficult problem. So much on Singapore depended on native labour. It had evaporated at the docks. The men just did not appear. Day after day the Japanese came over and bombed the docks. Tamil coolies preferred to stay at home in safety rather than risk their lives for what was after all an infinitesimal wage. Soldiers had to be taken away from military duties to unload ships. Indian troops, like the Gurkhas, who were sometimes diverted to these tasks, did them with an ill grace. Fighting men, they felt, should not be obliged to do coolie work. Early on in the campaign, out of a total labour force of 12,000 men at the Naval Base, less than 800 sometimes were reporting for duty. And when the Navy eventually left Singapore, it disbanded what was left of its labour force—at a time when the Army and the Air Force were crying out for labour. The evaporation of labour caused great difficulties at the airfields. There were not enough men to fill up the numerous bomb-craters. The native crews of ships in the harbour began to desert. The British officer in command of the patrol vessels had to appeal for white volunteers to man his ships. There were many small steamers and launches in perfect condition that never left Singapore because the native crews had deserted and there were not enough white people to operate them. Shops began to board up their windows while the owners sought refuge in the country. Native staffs, whether in hotels or offices, dwindled steadily.

There was a widespread feeling of hopelessness about the situation. But there was never panic. Most of the white people and many of the Asiatics grimly went about their business despite the feeling of hopelessness that they had in their hearts.

Could able and inspiring leadership have altered this state of affairs? Perhaps the realities of the military situation were such that no leadership, however brilliant, could have made much difference one way or the other. The fact remains nevertheless that the leadership was neither able nor inspiring. It was a moment for a big man built on a big scale, someone who could cut through all the red tape and rally the people and fire them, if not with the confidence of victory, then at least with the spirit of dogged resistance. No big man emerged.

Three days after the siege began I called on the Governor. There had been some remarkable explosions that morning. Shells appeared to be falling in the gardens of Government House. After a few minutes the shelling ceased.

The Governor was very affable, as always. He was a short, rather stout man, with a red face, of a most sanguine temperament. I think he prided himself upon being a good mixer who could get on with all sorts of people. He took me out to see the shell-holes. A bank only a few yards from the window of his study was slightly pitted. The surface of the ground in one or two other places was scarred. The nearest point on the mainland from which the shells could have been fired was some ten miles away. This mysterious shelling of Government House remained a puzzle but it was generally thought that some Japanese guns had been firing at extremest range and their spent missiles, by some extraordinary fluke, happened to land near this particular target. With a certain pride the Governor told me that a large number of bombs had fallen in the grounds, many of them close to the house itself. He was undergoing just the same risks as everyone else and took refuge during raids in a simple dug-out such as most of the Europeans had in their gardens. The Japanese fifth-column was continuously sowing rumours that either Sir Shenton or Lady Thomas had just left Singapore by plane for India. Every three or

four days there was an indignant denial. There was no question-
ing the Governor's sticking power. He was one of those solid,
imperturbable, unimaginative Englishmen who would face up to
anything. He was photographed in his shirt-sleeves helping to dig
away the debris of bombed houses, as an answer to the rumour-
mongers.

We talked about many things, about civilian morale, about the
scorched-earth policy as it had been enforced up-country, about
Singapore's chances of withstanding a long siege, about the times
we were living in. He was puzzled why civilian morale was low
and why there was so much defeatism amongst the British. The
scorched-earth policy, he felt, had been very well enforced up-
country. Critics did not appreciate some of the difficulties the
officials were up against. He personally thought the officials had
done very well. He said that he was completely confident Singapore could withstand a long siege. There was enough food, enough
water, enough medical supplies, plenty of soldiers. We were living
in stirring times. Singapore would have an opportunity to write an
epic in imperial history, another Malta, another Tobruk. He was
glad he was in Singapore. He would not be anywhere else for anything in the world.

I am certain that he was sincere and that he genuinely believed
that Singapore could hold out. Perhaps he never allowed himself
to think of the alternatives. He had said himself in one of his early
broadcasts: 'Singapore must not, shall not fall.' Was it not a case
of *post hoc ergo propter hoc*? Because it would be an imperial
tragedy if Singapore fell, therefore it was strong enough not to
fall? There was a curious atmosphere of unreality about the
thinking of many people in Singapore.

The Governor was a good solid official who had spent much of
his life in administering our African colonies. He took his respon-
sibilities to the native population seriously and the Chinese leaders
knew that he would not let them down. He had that stolid British
doggedness. But he was not a realistic thinker or even a very clear-
headed one. He was sanguine to the verge of complacency. He had
risen to his position, not by virtue of any outstanding ability, but
by dint of long years of steady conscientious work. There was no
colour or forcefulness about him, nor much decisiveness. His

broadcasts to the people which he made quite frequently were solid, sound, rather dull, man-to-man performances. The Governor was the last man to rally people in a crisis and inspire them to suffering, sacrifice, and heroism.

When I left he came to the veranda outside his study with me. There was a curious black dot just above the horizon to the northeast. The Governor saw it before I did. It was a balloon, moored to the ground by a cable, which the Japanese were using as an observation post for their artillery. They used balloons several times across the straits, more (I think) as a taunt to us than anything else, to bring home to us how completely weak we were in the air.

It so happened that the same day that I called on the Governor there was a Press conference held by Lieutenant-General Percival. It was interesting to see the civilian and military leaders of Singapore so quickly one after the other. Percival was a tall, thin person, whose most conspicuous characteristics were two protruding rabbit teeth. General Percival had wanted to address all the local editors as well as the correspondents, but the officer charged with convening the conference forgot completely to inform the editors of all the vernacular Malay, Chinese, and Indian papers. In spite of this omission three or four times as many people turned up as were expected. In addition to the correspondents and local British editors, there were broadcasters, censors, public relations officers, representatives of the Ministry of Information, and the local Malayan Department of Information, and others. No arrangements had been made for the conference. We were shepherded into a long dark room and chairs were hastily brought from neighbouring offices. The majority of us had to stand. Percival came in and sat down at the far end of the table. He was evidently surprised to see so many people. He began to read from notes. He wanted to see the Press, he said, because many people thought that we did not intend to hold Singapore. He wanted to assure them to the contrary. We very definitely did intend to hold Singapore. And then he said, with a slightly nervous laugh, 'In any case it's doubtful if we could withdraw from Singapore even if we wished to.' He continued with what was an attempt to plead for the co-operation of the civilian elements in the population and to answer some of the questions which people were asking. It had become general knowledge, for example, that nearly all our fighter aircraft had been withdrawn to Sumatra together with some anti-aircraft artillery. A small token force of Hurricanes had been left behind in Singapore. People were asking why aircraft were withdrawn if we intended to hold Singapore. Percival explained that they would be able to operate more satisfactorily based on Palembang, and if the aircraft moved, some of the guns which protected their base had to go with them. He elaborated on the labour question, which was causing such difficulties, and asked for the support of the Press. Successful resistance, he said, would depend on whole-hearted co-operation between the military and civilian elements. The one could not fight properly unless the other continued to perform certain essential functions.

Much of what the General said was sensible. But never have I heard a message put across with less conviction, with less force. Afterwards there were questions, and long agonizing silences before the next question was put. It was embarrassing as well as uninspiring. I felt that the General not only did not know how to deal with a group of pressmen, but that he did not know how to deal with any group of men.

Percival was a man of considerable personal charm, if one met him socially. He was an able staff officer with a penetrating mind, although a mind that saw the difficulties to any scheme before it saw the possibilities. But he was a completely negative person, with no vigour, no colour, and no conviction. His personality was not strong, and as a leader he did not appeal either to the troops (to whom he was unknown except by name) or to the general public.

Both Thomas and Percival would have got by in times of peace and, after their terms in Singapore had expired, would have retired honourably to England. But they were not the men to handle the extremely ticklish situation which prevailed in Singapore. One cannot blame people for being what they are. Usually in times of crisis the static leadership is swept aside by dynamic leadership. If the Malayan campaign had lasted six instead of just over two months this would doubtless have happened both in the military and civilian spheres. But things moved so quickly in Singapore that there was never time for it to happen.

The Men at the Top

In my opinion the best of the senior military leaders was Gordon Bennett. He was a rasping, bitter, sarcastic person, given to expressing his views with great freedom. As a result he quarrelled with a good number of people. But he did have a forceful personality. He was imbued with a tough, ruthless, aggressive spirit. As a soldier he was unconventional, but one wanted an unconventional soldier to deal with an unconventional situation. He was passionately proud of his men and devoted to their interests. His men knew it and had confidence in him.

(Bennett's subsequent escape to Australia has been the subject of much discussion. I myself have never been able to make up my mind about it. Intellectually, I think it was the right decision. He fought until the capitulation, and, when the capitulation had gone into effect, he made good his escape, like many other men. There is nothing to show that he left before the capitulation or that he abused his privileges as a general to secure facilities which other men could not have obtained. His determination not to remain a prisoner can be interpreted as evidence of an aggressive personality that refused to accept surrender or internment. There is no doubt that it is of the greatest value to the Australian Government to have the services of a senior officer with actual experience of fighting the Japanese in the field. And yet I confess I have that sentimental, emotional feeling that a commanding officer should stay with his men through thick and through thin, through the victories and through the defeats. I remain open-minded on the question. The view one takes of his escape depends largely on the extent to which one is emotionally or intellectually inclined.)

I do not think that more dynamic leadership at the top would have made much difference to the eventual outcome once we were all back on the island. Like many other people I believed that the battle of Singapore had already been lost in Johore. But the fact remains that the leadership was of poor quality. It was as I have described it above.

That evening, about ten o'clock, I dropped in to see Rob Scott. He was in his office, still working. He had just forwarded to the Ministry of Information a 'Three-Year Plan for Propaganda', covering work all over the Far East, including occupied territories, and including propaganda liaison with the Americans, Australians,

Singapore
On the extreme right is Fort Canning, headquarters of the
Malayan Command

Sappers prepare a bridge for demolition in South Johore

Women and children evacuated from up-country
arrive at Singapore station

'Denying' to the Japanese a car which had been abandoned
at the dock-side by evacuees

Dutch, Chinese, and Indian Governments. He was in khaki uniform. He and all his staff had joined the Local Defence Volunteers and used to attend parades when they could. As usual he was smoking one of his cheap acrid Burma cheroots.

Rob was one of the outstanding young Britishers in the Far East. He was now thirty-five. He had come out to the Far East in the China Consular Service some twelve years previously. At once he was marked out, and for several years he was private secretary to Sir Miles Lampson, who was then British Minister in China. (It was before our Legation was raised to be an Embassy.) Thereafter he had a succession of interesting jobs, those special jobs which go to the good man in any service. I don't think he ever occupied a routine consular post. Later on, like many of the abler and more ambitious men in the China Consular Service, he switched to the commercial side and was seconded to the Department of Overseas Trade. When I first met him in Japan in the winter of 1938 he was working with Hall-Patch, Financial Adviser to our Embassies in China and Japan. When Hall-Patch went home on leave Rob took his place. He was in England when the war broke out in 1939 and was appointed by Sir John Pratt, then head of the Far Eastern section of the Ministry of Information, to be Director of the Far Eastern Bureau of the Ministry of Information. In other words he was to return to the East to organize British propaganda. It was a tremendously big and vitally important job. He had to start from scratch. There was absolutely no British propaganda organization in the Far East at all. Japan was sitting on the fence. Tokyo was stiff with German propagandists and Nazi agents of all kinds. We had to try to counteract their malign influence which was concentrated on luring Japan into the fray on Germany's side. British Press attachés were appointed. Very rapidly organizations sprang up at all the important points—Tokyo, Shanghai, Chungking, Hong Kong, Bangkok, Batavia—while work was also initiated in many lesser centres. It was Rob's task to supervise and co-ordinate the work of the different posts. He travelled continuously. At first his headquarters was in Hong Kong, later he moved it to Singapore. In my opinion our propaganda organization in the Far East, during the two years that preceded Japan's entry into the war was in many ways a most effective organization indeed. More than once it helped to delay Japan's entry into the war. That it was effective, indeed that it attained the scale it did, was due very largely to the energy and ability of Rob Scott.

In appearance he had a broad open face, a dark moustache, hair that was beginning to go grey. He was very Scottish both in voice and manner. I worked as his assistant for two months. It was a revelation to me. He was the most accessible person in the world. A constant stream of people came to see him. He brought to his work a tireless energy, an accurate and shrewd mind that was brimfull of ideas, great tact in dealing with people, so that all those who met him liked and respected him. When Sir George Sansom left for Batavia to join General Wavell's staff Rob took his place on the War Council. The latter body met daily under the Governor's chairmanship, its other members being General Percival, Air-Vice-Marshal Pulford (the Air Officer Commanding), Rear-Admiral Spooner (the Senior Naval Officer), and Mr. Bowden, the Australian Government Commissioner.

Rob was tired that evening. He had been working all day and most of the night for weeks and weeks. He was cheerful, and not the least bit depressed. I never knew him depressed. He was one of the few intelligent and completely honest people in Singapore who thought that we could hold the place, that is, hold it on certain conditions—by taking big risks with the air, and shoving in reinforcements, and putting in a real leader, and taking chances.

Rob was a man who could have handled the Singapore situation, or any situation, with complete competence, could have cut through the red tape, and told people where they got off, and given strength and confidence to the people round him. But he was still in his thirties. It was only by threatening to resign from the War Council that he secured, ten days before Singapore fell, the full control over Press and publicity and censorship channels for which he had long been asking.

He left Singapore on February 11th, three days before the surrender, with the few remaining members of his staff. His ship is known to have sailed, but it has not been heard of to this day. There were many ships sunk by Japanese bombers between Singapore and Batavia. Rob's ship was almost certainly one of them.

The Men at the Top

Survivors from other bombed ships were picked up in the water or succeeded in making their way to the shore. No survivor from Rob's ship ever turned up. It is possible that he is on one of the Dutch islands. It is possible that he is in the hands of the Japanese. It is possible that the ship went down with all hands. Nothing definite is known. He is a man that we can ill afford to lose. He would have risen to the very highest positions.

18

THE CHINESE AND THE DEFENCE OF SINGAPORE

There were over half a million Chinese in Singapore. They had made Singapore quite as much as the British had made it. They emerged, in my opinion, from the two months of warfare in Malaya with flying colours.

The Chinese community in Singapore had always been rent by internal differences, of language, politics, economic status. Shortly after the war started some fifty leaders of the different Chinese communities called on the Governor and told him that they had agreed to sink their common differences and to give every support to the local government in the prosecution of the war. Tan Kah-kee was prevailed upon to become their leader. He was the only Chinese who could command the allegiance of all sections of the Chinese community. He was a Chinese who had risen from a lowly position and who, during the course of his life, had made and lost several huge fortunes in tin and rubber. For the last four years he had been head in the South Seas area of the United China Relief Fund, the organization which remitted millions of dollars to the Chungking war chests and was one of that régime's main sources of foreign currency. There were big meetings held and manifestoes published in the Chinese papers calling upon all Singapore Chinese to help the war effort. (Tan Kah-kee left Singapore for India with his family before the siege began. No-one can blame him. He would have been the first Chinese in Singapore to be put up against a wall by the Japanese and shot.)

There were three main forces at work. Firstly, there was the Kuomintang party organization, the official organization of the Chungking régime. The Chinese Consul-General, Mr. Kao Ling-pai, was greatly assisted by an extremely able young Chinese, George Yeh, who was the representative in Singapore of the

164

The Chinese and the Defence of Singapore

Chungking Ministry of Information. Secondly, there was the Malayan Communist Party, which was almost entirely Chinese in composition and used to maintain through Hong Kong an efficient but highly secret liaison with the Chinese communists in the north-western provinces of China. It had been completely suppressed the previous year as a result of an attempt to organize a general strike throughout Malaya. The Malayan Communist Party now came into the open again, voicing its determination to give whole-hearted backing to the local government in this war against Fascist aggression. Knowing the great influence which the M.C.P. still wielded amongst the poorer sections of the Chinese population, the Government lifted the ban and gladly welcomed the co-operation of this organization which it had so recently suppressed. Large numbers of political prisoners were released from gaol. They became active at once, holding meetings, leading processions, publishing manifestoes in the papers, posting up stickers all over Singapore— 'Join the fight against German, Italian, and Japanese Fascism', 'Help to crush Japanese Aggression', and so forth. While doubtless sincere in their motives, the Chinese Communists perceived that they were also gaining another end. They had a magnificent opportunity to tighten their hold upon the Chinese working classes. Later, when that hold had been established, they would be able to revert to their former platforms with great effect.

Thirdly, there was the bulk of the Chinese population who had no particular interest in politics either of the Chungking or Communist variety. Perhaps their families had lived in Singapore for four or five generations. Perhaps they could not even speak Chinese. These people were prompted by a keen sense of civic duty to do what they could to help in the defence of Singapore. The crisis had come to this city which was their home through adoption. They felt they had to respond to this crisis. Moreover, they were threatened by an enemy who was also the enemy of their country of origin, who had been warring against their kith and kin in China for four and a half years. They were all sympathetic to Free China's cause and had been greatly stirred by her gallant struggle. Therefore they flocked to join all the passive defence services. They became air-raid wardens, or auxiliary firefighters, or ambulance drivers, or stretcher-bearers. And they did a very fine job of work.

It was the Chinese quarters that were hardest hit by the air raids. When bombs were dropped on the civilian parts of the town (which was comparatively rarely when one considers how frequently the bombers used to come over) most of the victims would be Chinese.

There were no air-raid shelters in Singapore, only dug-outs and slit trenches. There were no public shelters in the densely crowded Chinese quarters. Some months before the outbreak of war, when the local government was considering the question of shelters, it decided, on what grounds I know not, that the marshy nature of the land made the construction of deep shelters impracticable. Singapore would have to rely on slit trenches and dispersal into the country. Many of the trenches that I saw in the native quarters did admittedly begin to fill with water at a depth of two feet. But surely the construction of concrete shelters underground, or even surface shelters, would have been practicable. There were hills in and around Singapore city, there were even great masses of rock, into which tunnels could have been bored. To my mind the most fantastic thing that happened during the whole war in Malaya was the official announcement made by the Government, the day before the Japanese landed on the island, that it had decided to build concrete shelters for the general public, but mark you, only in places where it was not practicable to dig slit trenches.

The correspondents were never allowed in their messages to refer to the absence of proper air-raid shelters. Eventually, on February 4th, the senior air-raid warden in Singapore gave a broadcast talk in which he said:

'It's no use telling the people that Malta has had a thousand raids and they have stuck it, or that Chungking has had worse than we've had. These places have ideal shelters and we have nothing except drains and trenches.'

The censors had wanted to kill this passage in the talk. It was referred to Rob Scott, who passed it. We cabled it home. Three

The Chinese and the Defence of Singapore

days later the Government announced that it had decided to build public shelters.

If you were in a massive concrete building like the Cathay Building you felt fairly safe during a raid. Anywhere else in Singapore you felt unsafe. The jerry-built houses in which the Chinese lived were absolute death-traps. Fortunately I do not think that their inhabitants often realized how dangerous they were.

Three days after the war began I remember going for a stroll in the evening round the Chinese quarters to see how the Chinese were reacting to the outbreak of war. Wherever there was an open piece of ground, Chinese were at work digging trenches, making dug-outs. They were doing it quite spontaneously, with what shovels or picks they happened to have, with what timber or corrugated iron they could find lying about. Their friends were standing round commenting on the efforts of the diggers, comparing the respective merits of the different types of trench. Some were open, some covered in, some straight, some zigzag, some below the surface of the ground, some (where the earth was marshy) above the surface. Old Chinese men, smoking their water pipes, wondered what it was all about. Children ran in and out among the legs of the bystanders, or played games in the trenches, thinking it the best game in the world. Mothers with small babies looked on apprehensively, uncertain what the future had in store for them, anxious not so much for themselves as for their little ones. There was a marvellous atmosphere of helpfulness and fellow feeling. One could not help admiring these people who, with so little direction from above, were doing what they could to prepare for the vague dangers that lay ahead of them.

After the siege of Singapore began there was an air raid on the civil airport at Kalang, from which the few remaining Hurricanes were operating. A large number of bombs fell wide of the mark. Some fell on a little Chinese settlement in a grove of coco-nut palms. They were the poorest of poor Chinese. The men would have been labourers or fishermen. They had gone out to work. Only the women and children were left at home. Their dwellings were simple sheds of timber and matting with an occasional piece of corrugated iron. Two or three bombs must have fallen right in the grove. The concussion sent a considerable number of the still green nuts tumbling down. The trouble about these sheds was that their owners had banked the walls with earth and also put earth on the roof. The blast caused the sheds to cave in like a house of cards. Timber, matting, corrugated iron, earth, all fell upon the unfortunate people inside. The air-raid wardens had already begun to dig the victims out when Rob Scott, Henry Stokes, and I arrived on the scene. They were an international gang—two Malays, a young Arab with a fez, some young Chinese, two or three Europeans. An ambulance had arrived. Two or three corpses were already laid out. We seized shovels and picks and helped in the work. Thirteen bodies, all of them women and children, were extracted from the debris.

For a long time we dug away at one particular place. Then a long board was lifted up and underneath was the body of a Chinese woman lying on her side with a small baby still at her breast. She must have been suckling it when the bombs fell. The baby was still alive. The woman's body had taken the weight of the mass that fell on her and somehow shielded the child. The mother's face was mutilated so that one could hardly recognize it. We laid the body out at the side. There was a group of children standing under the palms who had been some distance away playing when the disaster occurred. They were the children of the Chinese in the sheds. They were howling wildly. They could not make out what had happened. They only knew that it was something terrible. There was a little girl who was their leader. The woman with the baby whom we had dug out was her mother. She ran up, as we laid her out, crying desperately. We held her back. She continued to struggle and cry and was trying to say something through her tears. One of the Chinese wardens talked to her. It was some money. Her mother had some money tied in a sash round her waist. The little girl wanted the money. She was afraid that it might be lost or that someone might take it away. Rob Scott bent down and unfastened a red sash that was tied round the woman's waist, serving also as a belt for her trousers. He untied it. There was a purse wrapped up in the sash. He opened the purse and counted out four dollar notes and some small coins. It was the equivalent of about ten shillings. It was probably the family's entire worldly wealth. He gave it to the little girl. She snatched it, and, without saying a word, returned to the forlorn little group under the coco-nuts. She was mollified. Her crying became a snuffle. She looked at us with her watery eyes, sniffing slightly, and with great channels where the tears had run down her grubby little cheeks.

I could not help thinking that there was something typically Chinese about this little girl's action. There was nothing cynical or grasping about it. She was the product of generations of Chinese peasants, poor and thrifty, who had extracted a precarious living from the sea or from the soil. Their few dollars meant something to these poor people. They meant a lot to this little girl. At least she was saving something out of the disaster which had so suddenly overwhelmed the little community in the coco-nut grove.

On the ground floor of the Chinese Secretariat there was a large Chinese A.R.P. post and a medical auxiliary service first-aid station. The personnel were almost entirely Chinese. Often when there were night raids I used to walk down to it from the Po Leung Kuk Home. It was only a quarter of a mile away. Wardens would telephone in from other posts in that area and say where the bombs had dropped and where ambulances were required. Drivers and stretcher-bearers were all standing by in the Secretariat and would immediately go out and search for victims in the ruins. The wounded would be brought in and given immediate treatment. If they were very seriously wounded they would be sent to one of the hospitals on the island. If they were only lightly wounded, they would be sent home after receiving treatment. Camp beds were ranged in rows in one of the rooms. On a bad night there would be fifty or sixty people lying on them. The doctors were Chinese practitioners who had volunteered for this work. There were two or three trained European nurses but the rest of the nurses were all trim young Chinese girls, very neat in their white uniforms. There was also a canteen run by Chinese girl volunteers, serving tea and coffee and biscuits, for the work was carried on all day and all night. The Chinese in charge of the post was a young school-teacher. He was an altogether admirable person, efficient, capable, calm, strict with the people under him. His second-in-command was an enormous fat Chinese. His profession was that of a dealer in goldfish and fancy Chinese fish. The drivers and stretcher-bearers and telephonists and demolition men were mostly young Chinese in their teens or early twenties coming mostly from the shopkeeping classes. They were keen as mustard on the job. They had tin hats and simple sensible uniforms and used to feel tremendously important. They were doing a job that was important and necessary and also quite exciting. Of course there were shirkers and cowards among them. There are in every organization. But on the whole these young Chinese, both the women and the men, plunged into their work with a zest and a gusto that were deserving of the highest praise. In all the passive defence services the bulk of the personnel were Chinese. They contributed their quota nobly.

Early on in the war a Chinese Mobilization Council was formed under the chairmanship of Tan Kah-kee. It did excellent work. It did what it could to help with the labour question. Every morning at seven, during the weeks before Singapore fell, Chinese labourers, recruited through the energy of members of the council, would foregather at certain fixed points in the city. They would then be dispatched in lorries to places where there was an especial shortage of labour. Perhaps 2,000 men were required for clearing away some bombed buildings, or 500 were required for digging trenches in one of the parks, or the Air Force wanted some work done on one of its airfields, or the Army had a lot of supplies that had to be moved. There was never a sufficient supply of labour available, and, as time went on, it steadily diminished. But the Chinese Mobilization Council made a gallant attempt to cope with the problem.

At what date it was decided to call for Chinese volunteers and to arm them for fighting, I do not know. I used to spend so much of my time at the front that I rather lost touch with developments on the island. It was certainly very late in the campaign. The first company of volunteers only moved up to take their positions in the fighting line some five days before the Japanese assaulted the island.

The call for volunteers provoked an immediate and widespread response. The volunteers were of all sorts, labourers and students, middle-aged men and boys in their teens. There were

The Chinese and the Defence of Singapore

several veterans of the China wars, including some men who had fought with the 19th Route Army in the fighting round Shanghai in 1932. Young girl Communists, fired by the example of women in Russia, volunteered for service in the front line, and were bitterly disappointed when they were only permitted to do Red Cross work. There were guerrilla experts from China, sent down to Singapore by the Chungking Government to teach guerrilla warfare. Most of the volunteers came either from the Kuomintang or from the Communist organizations. They were trained, and placed in formations, according to their political sympathies. There was one school where the Kuomintang adherents were trained, another where the Communists were trained. The officers were British but were not regular soldiers. They were mostly officials of the Malayan Civil Service, men from the Forestry Service and the Malayan Police, or tough young planters from up-country, all of whom could speak Chinese. They were a fine body of men. The commanding officer was a crackerjack of a fellow, Colonel Dalley, a man perhaps of forty-five, who had been a stormy petrel in the Police for many years. He was as tough as you could wish, and handled both his officers and the volunteers with the utmost skill. Much of his time was spent in composing differences. I went with him to the Communist training school one morning. One of the inspirers of the whole enterprise, a Chinese Communist whom Dalley told me he had been chasing unsuccessfully for many years, had a very long story to tell. I asked Dalley what it was all about. The Chinese apparently was most anxious to be made a general. Dalley coped admirably with this type of problem.

The first volunteers left for the front on February 5th. There were scenes of tremendous enthusiasm as truck-loads of them left the training school. There were speeches, loud cheering, waving of flags. As they left, they sang a song which had been specially written for the occasion:

'Arise, arise, those who do not want to be slaves. Build a new Great Wall with your flesh and blood.'

Several companies were in training but I doubt if more than

171

three ever took part in the fighting. On the afternoon of Sunday, February 8th, Yates McDaniel, Henry Stokes, and I drove out with Dalley to have a look at one of the two companies which had already taken up their positions. Also with us was a young British official from the Chinese Secretariat who had been living in the Po Leung Kuk Home. For weeks he had been itching to get into the army and do some real fighting instead of sitting at his desk in the Secretariat. But he was a member of the Malayan Civil Service, and, as such, subject to orders, and for a long time his chief would not release him. Three days previously, however, he had secured his release and with tremendous enthusiasm had joined Dalley's Desperadoes, as they were popularly known. He was with us now and was going to join one of the companies at the front.

For several days past the Japanese artillery fire had been steadily increasing in volume. They had evidently been bringing more and more guns, of all calibres, into action on the further shore of the Straits of Johore. Our twenty-five pounders kept hammering away at them. The noise of gunfire went on intermittently all day and all night.

The Chinese volunteers were in a mangrove swamp in the north-west sector of the island, between two of the Australian battalions. We parked the car under some trees and began to walk north through the rubber plantations. Shells were whining overhead. Several times there was a sudden whistling whine and a shell would fall not far from us with a loud explosion. Instinctively and automatically we flung ourselves headlong on the ground, trying, as Henry put it, to squeeze our bodies under our tin helmets without much success. I was windier that day than I had ever been before during the Malayan campaign. And if I was windy, who had been bombed and dive-bombed pretty frequently up at the front and broken in to noise, what must it not be like for the young official who was going up to the front for the first time? We came across some Australians in a rubber plantation. They had dug shallow trenches and were sitting in them. They were jittery, no mistake about it. Shells were whistling over their heads. A few had burst near them. One had fallen near a trench killing two men and wounding three. We came across a party with a young

Australian soldier from one of the twenty-five-pounder batteries who had his leg blown off. He was groaning. His mates did not think that he would live. They were carrying him back to the aid post. Eventually, some 400 yards from the shore, we came to the headquarters of the Chinese company. They were located in a hut of corrugated iron where there was certain plant for processing rubber. The three British officers looked worn. This bombardment had gone on all night. They had not had much sleep. One of the platoons of the Chinese was resting in a hut close by. The men had no uniforms, but most had wrapped a cloth, turban-like, round their heads. They looked somehow like Chinese soldiers in old photographs of the Boxer rebellion. They were armed with all sorts of weapons, chiefly with shotguns. But they had only seven rounds of ammunition each and they asked Dalley to give them more. They were standing up to the bombardment well. They were amazingly cheerful. It was pouring with rain, and, while we were talking to the Chinese, it suddenly began to lighten and thunder. The uproar was enough as it was without the heavens also taking part in it.

We spent most of the afternoon in this sector. Dalley had some long conversations with his officers, with the Chinese, with the officers of the neighbouring Australian units. About five we made our way back, soaking wet. As we left the hut, I remember looking back and seeing my friend, who was staying there with the company, sitting disconsolately on a wooden box. He was pretty pale. I felt sorry for him. The front line, which he had been itching to get into for weeks, was different from what he had expected. Only six hours later the Japanese landed in that very sector. The Chinese company found itself in the very thick of the fighting, my friend with them.

One of the most remarkable experiments of the war in Malaya, the arming of these Chinese volunteers, began two years too late. They had what the Indian and Malay troops lacked, a personal venom against the Japanese, who for over four years had been killing their fellow-countrymen in China. They were inspired by something which nearly all the other fighting forces lacked. If they had been better trained and better equipped, and if we had had them when the war started, they might have played a vital

173

role in the fighting on the mainland. They had that mobility which the enemy had and we had not. They could have lived off the country and mingled with the people of the country. But the time to have started training them was two years before, not two weeks before, Singapore fell. And two years previously we had been thinking about Singapore in very different terms from those we were thinking in now.

Experience of the past five years has made us revise our opinion of the fighting qualities of the Chinese. They may not be good at mechanized, precision fighting, but there are many types of fighting at which they are very good indeed. There does not appear to be any such thing as a 'military nation' or an 'unmilitary nation'. The only thing that matters is that people should feel that the things which they are fighting and dying for are worth fighting and dying for, and that they should have a minimum of essential equipment.

When the Japanese came swarming on to the island, the Chinese volunteers put up a good fight, from what I have heard since. They fully justified the confidence which had been placed in them. But they were not able to make any difference to the progress of the struggle, and I fear that, as a result of their participation in the military struggle, the Chinese population was laid open to terrible reprisals once the Japanese armed forces were in full control.

19

THE LAST DAYS OF SINGAPORE

I went to bed about ten-thirty on the night of Sunday, February 8th. I was feeling very tired. The bombardment in the north that night had reached machine-gun tempo. Both the Japanese and ourselves seemed to be firing every gun in our possession. The rumble was not intermittent as it had been till now. It was continuous and sustained, like the rumble of wheels on a road. It was much louder, too, than it had been. The skyline to the north was an angry red, lit up by the flashes from the guns. It had been like this for the past few nights. Oil was ablaze at several points on the island. (There was enough oil on the island, so it was said, to fill Japan's wartime requirements for three months.) By day these fires cast a black pall of smoke over the island. By night they caused a dull red glow in the sky. The atmosphere was thick and murky. One never saw the sun except through a film of smoke. I thought of those Australian soldiers sitting in their shallow trenches under the rubber trees. I thought of my young friend who had gone up that day to join the Chinese company. Two nights before he had been sleeping in a camp-bed six feet away from mine.

A few planes flew over during the night. The sirens sounded the alert. Bombs were dropped in isolated places. They were raids intended to keep the inhabitants of Singapore awake and on edge. The little Chinese girls in the Po Leung Kuk Home stood up to all these alarms with admirable calm.

Early the following morning I went down to the press room in the Cathay Building and began to hammer out a story on the bombardment of the previous night. Hardly had I begun when Ian Fitchett came bursting in with the breathless news, which he himself had only just heard, that the Japanese had landed in the north-west of the island. Shortly afterwards the Singapore radio broadcast a short announcement stating that the enemy had

175

landed and that fighting was in progress. An official communiqué issued later by the Malayan Command said that offensive action was being taken to 'mop up' the enemy. Again that unfortunate term, which had been used in one of the first communiqués describing the fighting round Kota Bahru, suggested that the Japanese attack was merely a slight infiltration of troops who had slipped across in boats under cover of darkness, not an all-out large-scale assault.

During the course of the morning it was possible to piece together what had happened. The bombardment had been especially heavy between 7.0 and 11.0 p.m. the previous night. The Japanese had been firing every single gun they had, and had concentrated their fire on the north-western sector. Light, medium, and heavy guns, two-inch and four-inch mortars, had all stepped their fire, working from the shore inland and then back to the shore again. It must have been a grim experience for our men in that sector. They had already been subjected to five days of gunfire in a steadily increasing volume. I had observed the previous day what effect it had had on them. For four hours, from seven to eleven, the shells rained down on them. At eleven o'clock the attack began with the firing from the further shore of a green flare. It was pitch dark. The moon did not rise till nearly two. Our forces were dependent upon their searchlights to see anything coming across the water. The searchlights were switched on. It was the easiest thing in the world for Japanese machine-guns on the further shore to train their guns on to these searchlights and just keep firing until they hit the searchlights and knocked them out. One by one the searchlights were extinguished. The Japanese took off from the further shore in iron barges. They had brought them overland from the west coast. Each barge carried twenty or thirty steel-helmeted Japanese soldiers, with their machine-guns and mortars, with a good sprinkling, as always, of Rising Sun flags. Our machine-gunners down on the foreshore went into action. Although they were firing nearly blind, they trained their guns along the surface of the water. Bullets from the machine-guns struck sparks off the iron barges. They must have wrought considerable havoc. But they were not able to prevent the Japanese from reaching the island and leaping ashore. The barges went

The northern skyline of Singapore island as it was during
the ten days before the capitulation

McDaniel's ship after it had been attacked by
Japanese bombers

Yates McDaniel on a tropical island after his ship had been
bombed and sunk

Survivors from the bombed ship reach a small tropical island

back. They were powered, sometimes with aeroplane engines and propellers, sometimes with ordinary screws. They brought back more Japanese. Each time the landing was easier, for the first troops to land had already caused confusion amongst our forces on the foreshore. More and more Japanese came swarming onto the island. They had chosen their points of attack well. The two Australian battalions on whom fell the brunt of the fighting were the very battalions who had been hardest hit in the fighting on the mainland, the 19th and the 29th. Again the Japanese Intelligence service had served them well. The main attacks were made down the Kranji Creek in the north-west, and at Pasir Laba in the west, where the Japanese immediately began to press inland towards Tenga airfield.

When dawn broke, some three or four thousand Japanese shock troops had secured a firm foothold on the island. One column was pressing south from Kranji, the other was pressing east from Pasir Laba, in an attempt to cut off all our troops in the north-western sector. The danger of encirclement became so great that these troops were withdrawn and a rough line established between Kranji and Pasir Laba. The line was bulging inwards all the time. Fighting was in progress round the airfield.

Command reserves, including the Argylls (in the thick of it, as always), were being moved up. A counter-attack was scheduled for eleven o'clock. It was our last chance of driving the Japanese off the island. If that counter-attack failed (and there seemed small chance of its succeeding) then nothing on earth could save Singapore.

Henry Stokes and I drove up to A.I.F. headquarters off the Bukit Timah road. A short time before, a formation of Japanese bombers had flown over and given that area a pattern bombing, fortunately without damaging headquarters. There were some huge craters in the road north of Bukit Timah hill. We could see many Japanese dive-bombers operating over the Straits of Johore and over the western half of the island. Shells were falling on the outskirts of Singapore city.

Malayan Command was engaged on transferring its operational headquarters from Sime Road in the north-east part of the island to Fort Canning in the centre of the city. One of our conducting officers who went to see about arrangements for the evacuation of the war correspondents was curtly told that one correspondent and one ton of photographic equipment might leave; the rest were to stay put.

That afternoon I went out to the civil airport at Kalang from which our few remaining Hurricanes were operating. There were six machines in commission. A seventh was having its wheels repaired and might be available for service later. Never have I admired people more than I admired those boys. They were tired out. They had been flying infinitely longer hours than fighter pilots are supposed to fly. The strain was all too evident. But they stuck grimly to their task. They were doing what they could to harry the dive-bombers who were giving our ground troops such hell in the western part of the island. They had had a good bag that morning and had shot down three certainties, three probables, and several possibles. A young wing-commander was in charge. He cannot have been more than twenty-three. The others were lolling in easy chairs. They knew that they would have to go up in another half-hour or so. They were finding it difficult to relax. The most phlegmatic was a Canadian pilot who sucked philosophically at his pipe. He had joined an R.A.F. squadron at the beginning of the war. One of their number had not returned from that morning's operations. There was an atmosphere of tremendous tension amongst that little group. But I came away feeling that I had been amongst true heroes.

The airfield itself was pitted with craters. The planes often took off from the long asphalt road that ran alongside. There were two Hurricanes that had crash-landed by the side of the road. Other burnt-out hulks were littered about the field. The big hangars at the far end were charred ruins.

As we returned through the city there were queues outside the cinemas. I do not think that it was altogether complacency. I could understand that people should prefer to watch a film rather than sit around mopingly waiting for news of the fighting.

That evening it became quite obvious that whatever counter-attacks might have been made had failed. The Japanese were slowly pressing inland. Already they had occupied most of the western half of the island. Thousands more of them crossed onto the island during the night, bringing some of their field guns with them.

The next morning I bicycled out to the western part of the city. The rumble of artillery fire was continuous, and now it was mingled with the sharp sputter of machine-guns and the noise of rifle fire. Smoke from the burning oil-tanks hung low over the city. It was a fitting backdrop, during those grim days, to the sombre drama that was being enacted on the island of Singapore. Overhead, although we could not see them, the sun was shining and the sky was of deepest blue. Troops wandered through the streets. Some, with full battle kit and an air of purpose, were moving to take up new battle stations. Others were wandering, grimy, lost, leaderless, without orders. Military transport tore through the streets. The native population huddled together in doorways or sat in perplexed frightened groups under the trees in the parks and open spaces. There were several raids on the docks. Sometimes the sirens sounded. More often the first indication of a raid was the familiar vibrating drone of the big formations, or the firing of the anti-aircraft guns, or the thunderous roll as the bombs landed. The town was buzzing with the wildest rumours: that the Japanese had been pushed back into the sea, that their vanguards had reached the botanical gardens only three miles north of the city, that parachutists had tried to seize the broadcasting station, that American troops had landed at Penang. The little white puffs of bursting anti-aircraft shells often gave rise to reports that parachutists were descending.

At midday the Governor came out with a statement which (so it seemed to us correspondents) for sheer fatuity exceeded anything in the numerous speeches, messages, orders of the day, and official pronouncements which had been made on the subject of Singapore. 'We are all in the hands of God,' Sir Shenton declared, 'from whom we can get comfort in our anxieties and strength to play the man and help one another in all the ordeals which are to come.' Rob Scott had had to drive him back from the meeting of the War Council that morning. His native chauffeur had run away.

That afternoon I stood on the veranda in the Cathay Building looking out over the desolate spectacle that Singapore now presented. Only a quarter of a mile away, on its little hill, stood Fort Canning, headquarters of the Malayan Command. Shells began to fall on the lower slopes of the hill. In one place they started a small fire. The Japanese had reached the outskirts of Bukit Timah, only five miles away from the city. I gave Singapore thirty-six hours.

I confess I felt somewhat apprehensive. It was not the fear of bombs but the fear of delaying my departure from Singapore too late that prompted me to go down to the docks and investigate the shipping situation for myself. Gordon Bennett had already advised the official Australian correspondent to get out while he could.

I bicycled down through the parks round the Cathedral. There stood the remains of a Navy 0 which had been placed on public display in the early days of war. Down at Clifford Pier there was appalling confusion. There were still women and children on Singapore who had not been evacuated. Someone had told them to be down at Clifford Pier at 3.0. But there was no-one at the pier to tell them what to do. There were no launches to take them out to the evacuation boat. Then the sirens went. People scuttled for whatever shelter they could find. The anti-aircraft guns along the front began to fire. Many people thought that the bombs had begun to drop. It was another raid on Keppel Harbour one mile to the south-west. The planes droned off. People reassembled. Then a message came through to say that they were to embark not at Clifford Pier but at Keppel Harbour. Most of them picked up their suitcases wearily and began to trudge towards the docks. There were many touching scenes. There was a young officer and his wife. They had not been married long. He had been in an oil company and was now in the volunteers. For a long time she had refused to leave him, maintaining that she preferred internment to evacuation. But now he had prevailed upon her to go. He had to stay and fight.

People were driving down to the docks and then just abandoning their cars by the dockside. They could do little else. They could not sell their cars. In most cases their chauffeurs had run away.

There were several ships anchored out in the roads. I hired a Chinese sampan which took me out to them. The first was a small Dutch cargo vessel. I climbed aboard, asked the skipper where he was going, and whether he could take another passenger. He referred me to a Dutch naval commander. The ship was taking the few remaining Dutch nationals in Singapore, including four naval officers, to Batavia. The commander was willing to take me. But the ship was sailing very soon. I decided to take this opportunity.

I had given Singapore thirty-six hours. But it was 127 hours before fighting ceased. There is no doubt that many of the British troops, as the Japanese themselves admitted, fought bravely in what they knew was a hopeless situation. But the Japanese advanced steadily from the north-west. They repaired the causeway and brought their medium tanks over. Their artillery drew ever closer to the city. The British were forced back into the eastern half of the island.

An invitation to our Command to surrender was dropped on February 11th by an aeroplane. The leaflets were signed by Yamashita and began: 'I advise immediate surrender of the British forces at Singapore, from the standpoint of *bushido*, to the Japanese Army and Navy forces, which have already dominated Malaya, annihilated the British Fleet in the Far East, and acquired complete control of the China Sea and the Pacific and Indian Oceans, as well as south-western Asia.'

The British forces on Singapore, like the British forces at Hong Kong, ignored the invitation to surrender and fought doggedly on. But the position became more and more desperate. The enemy gained control of the two reservoirs in the centre of the island. The main broadcasting station in the middle of the island was blown up to prevent its falling into the hands of the enemy. The Naval Base was occupied. The troops were pounded unceasingly by dive-bombers, by big formations of bombers, by the enemy's artillery. They were completely exhausted. They had been fighting with little rest for nearly a week. Capitulation was inevitable. Finally, in the early afternoon of Sunday, February 15th, three British officers (led by that very man who in Kuala Lumpur some weeks previously had talked about the 'spot of bother' on the Slim River) advanced towards the Japanese lines waving a white flag. They were escorted through the Japanese lines to Yamashita's headquarters which were located in the Ford Motor Company's factory on the Bukit Timah road. A meeting was arranged.

181

The Last Days of Singapore

During the afternoon, a party of senior officers motored to the Ford factory. The motor-car bore a large Union Jack and a white flag. The meeting took place. Over 70,000 British troops, together with their guns, their transport, their equipment, surrendered to the enemy. It was the biggest military disaster that had overtaken British arms since the war started on September 3rd 1939.

For some hours, by the terms of the capitulation agreement, order in Singapore city was maintained by British *and* Japanese troops. The latter then completed their occupation. Tokyo radio announced that immediately they set about clearing up 'seditious elements' in the city. (One thought of those Chinese volunteers who had fought by the side of the British, all those Chinese in Singapore who for one reason or another were in the black-lists of the Japanese and Wang Ching-wei agents.) The British forces were interned in the barracks at Changi in the extreme east of the island. British civilians were rounded up and confined to the Sea-view Hotel to the east of the city. A curtain of silence has since descended upon Singapore and its thousands of internees.

Singapore was renamed by the Japanese 'Shonan' island, 'Light of the South'. The character for 'sho' is the same as in 'Showa', the name given to the era of the reign of the present Japanese Emperor. 'Nan' is the character for the south.

In Japan the fall of Singapore was the occasion of nation-wide rejoicings. In Britain, and in those countries which were her allies, the fall of Singapore, coinciding as it did with the escape of the German battleships from Brest, marked one of the blackest moments in this long struggle, which has known so many black moments, and will know many more, before it is fought to a successful conclusion.

20

AFTERTHOUGHTS

The sea was a deep Mediterranean blue. A light breeze rippled the surface of the water. As I looked towards Singapore from the ship, the evening sun was throwing up into high relief the buildings along the water front: Union Building, where P.R. had had its first headquarters, the stately building of the Hong Kong and Shanghai Bank, the massive Post Office, the old-fashioned red-brick Government Offices, the white cupola of the recently built Supreme Court, the tall spire of the Cathedral, the thirteen-story Cathay Building, where I had lived and worked. Black smoke hung fatefully over the whole island. There were fires in six or seven different places. At one point a great white column rose up above the layer of black smoke, like the eruption of a volcano. From the ship I could see something that I had not seen for days—the sky above Singapore Island. It was of purest blue, as if the heavens were supremely indifferent to the human tragedy that was being played out on the expanse of mangrove swamp that had become, in little over a hundred years, one of the great cities and ports of the world.

The rumble of artillery fire was wafted across the water. I thought of the desperate struggle that was still in progress— in the rubber plantations, on the tarred roads, in the gardens of those stately residences where the British lived, in the native villages, perhaps by this time in the streets of the city itself.

At dusk anchor was weighed, and the little ship began to pick its way slowly and carefully through the minefields which beset Singapore on all sides. I looked back on the island. It was a long, low expanse of green, so flat in some places that the land seemed to merge imperceptibly with the sea. In the centre there were gentle rolling hills. The genius and foresight of one Englishman had perceived the enormous significance of this then almost unin-

183

habited island. He had had the energy to transform his dream into reality.

Always, when I think of Singapore during its final days, I think of the fires and the clouds of smoke that hung over the city. For a long time that night we could see the dull glow which the fires caused in the sky over Singapore.

Near a small island a launch came out to take off the pilot. Three Australian soldiers who had come aboard the previous night also climbed down into it to go ashore.

Among our passengers were two seamen off the *Empress of Asia* which had been bombed and sunk by Japanese bombers just off Singapore a short time previously. No-one had looked after them in Singapore or assumed responsibility for them. Eventually they had just taken the matter into their own hands and boarded a ship. They had no clothes except what they stood up in. They had lost their papers of identification when the *Empress* went down.

Early the following morning we anchored about one mile from a small tropical island. The captain decided to halt here for the day. For many days past Japanese bombers had been active bombing ships plying between Singapore and Batavia. The northern stretch of the Banka Straits had already come to be known as 'Bomb Alley'. The little island was off the beaten track. It was safer, thought the captain, to spend the day here and then to sail down the straits under cover of darkness.

Three times that day Japanese planes flew overhead. But they did not molest us. We looked up into the sky anxiously and watched them pass over the ship. We had six huge crates containing Glenn Martin bombers lashed to the hatches and the decks. The ship had left Batavia with them over two weeks before to take them to Singapore. It had not proved possible at Singapore to uncrate them and put them into commission, so they were being taken back to Java. Above the crates, but covered with a tarpaulin, was the fuselage of a Glenn Martin belonging to the Dutch Air Force which had crash-landed at Singapore. Damage had been slight and it was being taken to Java to be repaired there and put into commission again. The crates were very conspicuous from the air and the captain decided that he would try to camouflage them with foliage.

Afterthoughts

Volunteers were called for and two of the ship's boats were lowered. There were two Dutch naval lieutenants on board, magnificent men, extremely good-looking. Each took charge of one of the boats. It was a long row to the shore. Our crew was composed of Hollanders, Swiss, and Czechs.

The island was of the kind that one thought existed only in the pages of sentimental novels. The surf was breaking on a stretch of white sand. Ferns and coco-nut palms grew along the shore. Further back was the dense variegated foliage of a tropical jungle. A native came rowing by in a canoe to see what was happening. We stripped naked and bathed after our exertions in the boat. Then we seized axes and *parangs* and began to chop down bushes and trees which we loaded into the boats. After an hour we returned. It was a long pull back to the ship. The Malay seamen festooned the foliage round the masts, the crates, and the funnels. It broke up the outlines and served its purpose.

We lay at anchor till the evening and then again resumed our voyage. Even now, as I looked back over the little island, Singapore would not allow itself to be forgotten, even though it was some 120 miles away. The great column of white smoke was still visible. The volcano was still erupting. Singapore was dying. It was a funeral pyre in keeping with the tremendous significance of what had happened.

I pondered many problems during that voyage from Singapore to Batavia.

The implications of the fall of Singapore were so vast. Now the Indian Ocean lay open to the Japanese fleet. Both Burma and the Indies were exposed to attack. West of Burma was India, south of the Indies were Australia and New Zealand. The Indies were now denied those precious few weeks in which to take delivery of those materials, especially planes, which they had long ordered and long paid for. Every day that Singapore stood was a day gained to the Allies. It was not a question of Singapore holding out indefinitely. Two months would have made a great difference, perhaps a vital difference, to the Allied position both in Burma and the Indies. Singapore was a corner-stone whose retention by the Allies was essential to the maintenance of the whole allied defence system in the south-west Pacific. Take away the corner-stone and the whole structure would come toppling down.

For some weeks past the fighting in Malaya had partaken of the nature of a denying operation. Singapore was no longer much use to us as a base for offensive naval and aerial operations against the enemy. But, as long as we retained it in our possession, even if we could not use it, there would not be the necessity of fighting to recapture it. To recapture a place is always harder than to retain it.

How had Singapore, whose garrison had been reinforced by one whole British division, yielded so easily to the Japanese assault? Even those of us who were never very confident of its strength never expected it to go like this.

The irony of the situation was that, having enjoyed a numerical superiority all down the mainland, the Japanese secured their foot-hold on Singapore with a numerical inferiority. In the early stages of the fighting on the island some of the correspondents talked about 100,000 troops being hurled against Singapore. But I doubt if there were more than two Japanese divisions engaged during the vital first three days of the fighting, although more may have been thrown into the fray later.

Although there were between 70,000 and 80,000 British troops on Singapore, not more than 45,000 of them were (in my opinion) combat units. If one reckoned as vulnerable territory the entire northern shore line of Singapore and included also strips on the east and west which were not far from the mainland, there were some forty-five miles of shore line where landings might be attempted. Out of the total number of front-line units, some had to be allotted to Command reserves, some had to be in readiness to deal with possible parachute landings, a form of attack to which Singapore was well adapted. There were, therefore, well under one thousand men to each mile of shore line. I remember thinking, during my visits to sectors in the north (at the Naval Base, for example, at Seletar, at this end of the Johore causeway, at Kranji), how very few troops there appeared to be up in these areas when one considered the large number who were known to be on the island. Undoubtedly the Japanese concentrated very considerable strength at the two points where they made their fiercest assaults (at Kranji and Pasir Laba), and it is possible that in these two places they enjoyed once more a local numerical superiority. The important objective for the Japanese was to secure a foothold. Once they had secured a foothold, they could then pour troops across the Straits of Johore, and continue to maintain a favourable ratio in numbers as the front widened and more British troops were thrown into the fighting. The Japanese were able to concentrate their strength at one or two points. Our strength was dispersed over 220 square miles. They had also that great advantage which always belongs to the attacker, the advantage of being able to choose where, when, and how they would strike.

The barrage which preceded the assault was not heavy in volume by comparison with some of the artillery barrages of the Great War. But it was slightly different in kind in so far as the men who had to stand up to it had little or no protection. It was possible to dig trenches on the rising ground, which gave a certain protection, but it was not possible to dig down on the foreshore near the water's edge where the searchlight operators and the machine-gunners and many of the troops had their stations. The earth was swampy and trenches filled immediately with water.

The bulk of our forces had participated in a long, exhausting, and thoroughly dispiriting action all down the mainland. Losses had been heavy, especially amongst the best troops. The reinforcements, although substantial, were mostly not seasoned troops, and they were plunged into some bloody fighting, of a particular kind, very soon after they arrived. Most of our forces on the island were, to use their own expression, thoroughly 'browned off', especially with continuous unopposed bombing and machine-gunning from the air. If they had occasionally seen our fighters attacking these Japanese planes or dive-bombing the Japanese ground troops, they would have stood up to things better.

The battle of Singapore has been described as a battle of flesh and blood against equipment. There are many elements of truth in this description. Reinforcements of men arrived. There were not enough men, it is true. But it was not primarily men who were wanted. It was above all fighter planes. It was tanks. (A few arrived during the final days but we never had any on the mainland.) It was more anti-tank guns, more anti-aircraft guns. It was

Afterthoughts

heavier guns which would have enabled us to put up a barrage comparable to that which the Japanese played upon us. It was more tommy-guns, more automatic weapons.

Not one but many factors were responsible for the fall of Singapore. There were the inherent weaknesses in the situation. It was a campaign fought on the military plane alone. Not a little of the Japanese success was due to the efficient way in which the military, aerial, and naval arms all co-operated, and blended to form one striking force of great power. There was also the question of relative numerical strength. Most important single factor, there was the enemy's almost unchallenged control of the air. It enabled him to gain control of the sea. It exerted a most powerful effect on the morale of our forces.

Troops will fight well if they know that they are well equipped. It is one of the strengths of the German and Russian armies that the men know that their equipment is the best available. They have a tremendous pride in their weapons. To go into battle knowing that the material terms are equal is to have a great feeling of confidence. But troops will also fight well without this condition as long as certain other conditions prevail. Was it not Napoleon who said that the material is to the psychological as one is to three? And another Frenchman who said that there are no bad soldiers, only bad officers? Not that the officership in Malaya was bad. Far from it. There were many able officers. But there was a softness and lack of forcefulness at the very top which made itself felt from the top downwards. The material of the men was potentially good. Something was lacking to realize those potentialities.

The tragedy of Malaya, to one who went through it, was that, in spite of the catastrophic nature of the débâcle, there were so many men who gave of their utmost, sweated under the burning sun in swamp and jungle, worked day and night at their desks for weeks, stood firm when all others wavered, saw clearly the odds against them but faced them courageously and cheerfully, gave of their blood and their limbs and their lives. The memory of many of them recurs to me when I think of the campaign. My Australian cousin, who, when he heard that the Command had decided upon capitulation, broke down completely (so I was told by one of

his brother officers who escaped) and wept uncontrollably. Major
Anderson, the senior Intelligence officer up-country, who did
some brilliant and daring work in the field in Johore and then was
ambushed by some Japanese and killed. Colonel Robertson, killed
while commanding his battalion on the Slim River. Patrick Don,
whom I had known at Winchester, also ambushed by the enemy
and (so it was reported) seriously wounded. Dickinson, head of the
Malayan Police, an outstandingly able person. Tony Tremblett
and Hockenkow, of the Chinese Special Branch of the Police, two
brilliant young Englishmen in their early twenties. McKerron, a
senior member of the Malayan Civil Service, Chief Censor when I
first met him, a vigorous, receptive, able administrator. The
young Malayan Civil Servant whom we left in the north-western
sector that fateful evening. The young Scottish Forestry officer
who used to go with the commando units behind the enemy's
lines. There were men of every age and every profession—officials,
police officers, planters, tin-mining engineers—who strove man-
fully to stem the tide. For every case of personal effeteness or
ineffectiveness that I came across in Malaya there were two of
personal toughness and courage. It is not right that what these
men did should be forgotten, simply because the general public
would prefer to forget Malaya and Singapore.

Whatever happens in the future, there can be no return to the
status quo in Malaya. If the fundamental economic causes of
modern wars are to be removed, then the natural resources of this
world (of which Malaya was such a rich repository) must be made
more freely and justly available to the nations that need them.
This end can only be achieved, in my opinion, by some sort of
international control, or by a joint Anglo-American control impar-
tially and responsibly administered in the interests of all, not
simply in the interests of one group of powers. Japan, unless her
power is broken, is certain to follow in Malaya a rigidly exclusivist
policy, infinitely more exclusivist than anything the British ever
practised, which can only lead to another war.

I came away from Singapore in an angry, tempestuous mood,
feeling that Malaya and Singapore had deserved to go; that, if the
British ran the rest of their Empire as they had run things recently
in Singapore, then they did not deserve to have an empire at all;

that the virtue had gone out of the British; that the rot had been something organic, and that we had had the leaders we had had because we had been worthy of nothing better. Time softened this mood, and I began to see the whole campaign more dispassionately, more in perspective. But I felt it strongly at the time, and I feel it strongly now, that those strata of the population of Great Britain who had been administering our colonial empire for the past twenty years had been found gravely wanting in the very qualities which had gained us an empire. And not only those who had been administering our colonial empire, but also those who had been residing in it and making profits out of it, and those others who had been responsible for the formulation of its policies and the ensuring of its defence. They had been found wanting in vigour, in ruthlessness, in aggressiveness. They had allowed themselves to go soft. They had had power but had been afraid to use it. They had drifted complacently along. Those necessary qualities of greatness are not lost. I get the impression (from the other side of the world) that there is a new upsurge of them amongst the people of Great Britain. We must incorporate them into our national life if we are to maintain our greatness as a nation and reassert our power in the East.

On the human plane, that is the simple, short moral of the Malayan campaign. On the material plane, the moral is also simple and short. The campaign demonstrated above all things the importance of the aerial arm in modern warfare, especially when it is used in close conjunction with the naval and military arms. This aspect of the campaign was extremely depressing to those who studied it on the spot. But from it we should take our chief hope for the future. Once we can establish overwhelming superiority in the air (and with American production I am confident that we can establish it), then we shall be able, with much greater effect, to do to the Japanese what they have been doing to us—to sink their capital ships and aircraft carriers, to smash up their big formations of bombers and claw them down from the skies, to prevent their fighters from taking to the air, to blitz their airfields and destroy their planes as they lie ranged on the ground, to hammer their sea and land lines of supply, to bomb their transports as they lie at anchor, to set their godowns and oil tanks on fire. But the most

Afterthoughts

telling place to hit Japan is not on the periphery of her conquests, but at the very centre of her national life. Never was there a country more vulnerable to aerial attack than Japan. Incendiary raids on the sprawling industrial centres of Japan would enormously disrupt her whole wartime economy. They would also affect the spirit of the people. For four and a half years Japanese bombers have been raining down death and destruction upon the defenceless millions of China. But the Japanese people have had no conception of what has been taking place in China. They have only known the indirect consequences of war, loss of relatives and shortage of commodities. They have borne them cheerfully. Never, until the mysterious raids in April, were they called upon to face up to the direct consequences. Knowing the Japanese, I should expect them to stand up to bombing raids with the same stoicism that they always display in the face of natural disasters. But only then will they perceive the true implications of the career of conquest on which they have embarked with such ardour. Japan is a country that has never known war, as Chungking has known it, as London has known it, as Moscow has known it, as Berlin is getting to know it. Until she has a taste of it, there can be no change in her present militant temper.

Only one thing impresses the Japanese as they are to-day—superior force. When we can amass this superior force (as assuredly we shall one day be able to amass it), we should strike hard at the centre of the nation's life, and thus shake the very foundations on which the whole vast structure ultimately rests.

INDEX

Index

Casualties, 49, 68, 139, 168
Catalina boat, 11
Cathay building, 47, 167, 175, 179, 183
Celebes, 18
Censorship, 15, 73, 146, 147, 166
Census figures, Malayan, 28
Changi, 182
Chiang Kai-shek, 40
Chicago Daily News, 73
Chicago Tribune, 72
China, communism in, 165, 171; Consular Service, 161; Squadron, 59, 152
China Sea, 18
Chinese, air-raid victims, 166; civil defence workers, 165–71; fighting qualities, 174; in Malaya, 30; Mobilization Council, 170; volunteers in Singapore, 170 sqq.
Chungking, 11, 41, 70, 129, 161, 164, 165, 166, 171, 191
Churchill, Rt. Hon. W., 44, 95, 154
Clifford Pier, 180
Collins, J., 121
Columbia Broadcasting System, 15, 73
Combined Services Public Relations Unit, 60
Communiqués, 49, 56–7, 145–6
Copra, 18
Correspondents, 72 sqq., 105, 121, 142
Craigie, Sir R., 53
Crocodiles, 25–6
Crosby, Sir J., 56

Daily Express, 72; *Herald*, 72; *Mail*, 72; *Telegraph*, 72
Dai Nippon, 45
'Daisy-cutter' bombs, 91
Dalley, Col., 171–3; 'Dalley's Desperadoes', 172
Datsun car, 88
Dickinson, 189
'Diggers', 12
Dive-bombing, 26, 68, 73, 90, 172, 181
Dogras, 75, 138
Don, P., 189
Duff Cooper, Rt. Hon. A., 13, 59, 60, 99, 154
Durdin, T., 72, 112
Dutch East Indies, 130
Dutch life in Malaya, 38–9
Dutch rule in Indies, 38

East Indies, 25
East Surrey Regiment, 75
'Economic' weapon, 41

Empress of Asia, 184
Endau, 14, 135
Enveloping tactics, 43
Eurasians, 28, 36, 37
Evacuation of Batu Pahat, 132; of Penang, 69–71
Evans, Dr., 69

Fairhall, T., 72
Fawcett, Brig.-General, 136
Federated Malay States, 33, 70, 74
Ferguson Stewart, Capt,, 136
Fifth Column, 5, 43, 78, 116
Fighter planes, 19, 39, 42, 88–9, 92
Fitchett, I., 72, 175
Floating Docks, 12, 151
Flying Fortresses, 93
Foochow, 29
Food situation, 80, 147–8
Formosa, 21
Fort Canning, 147, 177, 180
Fraser, C., 72
French Fleet, 19, 20
Fuji-San, 53
Future of Malaya, 189

Gallagher, O. D., 60, 72
Gas, 79, 136
Gemas, 110, 119, 120, 126
Georgetown, 68
German, influence, 42–4; personnel in Malaya, 105–7, 121; propaganda in Far East, 161
Gotemba, 53
Grik road, 100
Guard, H., 72, 146
Guerrillas, 171
Gulf of Siam, 14, 59, 67, 152
Gurkhas, 12, 75, 76, 83, 85, 109–10, 155

Hainan, 29, 32
Hall-Patch, 161
Halmahera, 18
Heath, Lt.-Gen. Sir L., 98, 137
Hiroshige, 53
Hitler, 42, 46, 131
Hokusai, 53
Holidays in Japan, 52–3
Hong Kong, 12, 16, 19, 137, 161, 181
Hudsons, 92, 135
Hull, Mr. Cordell, 46
Hurricanes, 92, 94, 135, 140, 152, 167, 178

Imperial Guards, Japanese, 127
Incendiary bombs, 68
'Incident', the, 63

Index

Index

Index